HiSET Math Exercise Book

2022

A Comprehensive Workbook
+ HiSET Math Practice Tests

By

Reza Nazari

Effortless Math provides unofficial test prep products for a variety of tests and exams. It is not affiliated with or endorsed by any official organizations.

All inquiries should be addressed to:
info@effortlessMath.com
www.EffortlessMath.com

ISBN: 978-1-63719-168-2

Published by: **Effortless Math Education Inc.**

For Online Math Practice Visit www.EffortlessMath.com

Welcome to
HiSET Math Prep
2022

Thank you for choosing Effortless Math for your HiSET Math test preparation and congratulations on making the decision to take the HiSET test! It's a remarkable move you are taking, one that shouldn't be diminished in any capacity.

That's why you need to use every tool possible to ensure you succeed on the test with the highest possible score, and this extensive math workbook is one such tool.

If math has never been a strong subject for you, don't worry! This book along with our online HiSET Math resources will help you prepare for (and even ACE) the HiSET Math test. As test day draws nearer, effective preparation becomes increasingly more important. Thankfully, you have this comprehensive workbook to help you get ready for the test. With this book and Effortless Math online resources, you can feel confident that you will be more than ready for the HiSET Math test when the time comes.

First and foremost, it is important to note that this book is a workbook and not a textbook. Every lesson of this practice book was carefully developed to ensure that you are making the most effective use of your time while preparing for the test. This up-to-date book reflects the 2022 test guidelines and will put you on the right track to hone your math skills, overcome exam anxiety, and boost your confidence, so that you can have your best to succeed on the HiSET Math test.

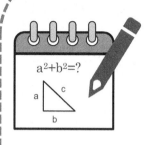

This exercise book will:

☑ Explain the format of the HiSET Math test.

☑ Describe specific test-taking strategies that you can use on the test.

☑ Provide HiSET Math test-taking tips.

☑ Help you identify the areas in which you need to concentrate your study time.

☑ Offer exercises that help you develop the basic math skills you will learn in each section.

☑ Give **2 realistic and full-length practice tests** (featuring new question types) with detailed answers to help you measure your exam readiness and build confidence.

This resource contains comprehensive practice questions and exercises that you will need to prepare for the HiSET Math test. You'll get numerous skill building exercises as well as tips and techniques on how to prepare for your HiSET math test.

In addition, in the following pages you'll find:

➢ **How to Use This Book Effectively** – This section provides you with step-by-step instructions on how to get the most out of this comprehensive study guide.

➢ **How to study for the HiSET Math Test** – A six-step study program has been developed to help you make the best use of this book and prepare for your HiSET Math test. Here you'll find tips and strategies to guide your study program and help you understand HiSET Math and how to ace the test.

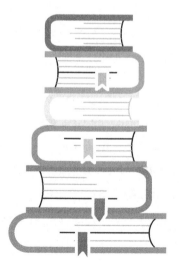

➢ **HiSET Math Review** – Learn everything you need to know about the HiSET Math test.

➢ **HiSET Math Test-Taking Strategies** – Learn how to effectively put these recommended test-taking techniques into use for improving your HiSET Math score.

➢ **Test Day Tips** – Review these tips to make sure you will do your best when the big day comes.

Effortless Math's HiSET Online Center

Effortless Math Online HiSET Center offers a complete study program, including the following:

✓ Step-by-step instructions on how to prepare for the HiSET Math test

✓ Numerous HiSET Math worksheets to help you measure your math skills

✓ Complete list of HiSET Math formulas

✓ Video lessons for all HiSET Math topics

✓ Full-length HiSET Math practice tests

✓ And much more...

No Registration Required.

Visit **EffortlessMath.com/HiSET** to find your online HiSET Math resources.

How to Use This Book Effectively

Look no further when you need a study program to improve your math skills to succeed on the math portion of the HiSET test. Each chapter of this comprehensive workbook will provide you with the knowledge, tools, and understanding needed for every topic covered on the test.

It's imperative that you understand each topic before moving onto another one, as that's the way to guarantee your success. You can use Effortless Math online course (a free course) to find examples and a step-by-step guide of every math concept in this workbook to better understand the content that will be on the test. To get the best possible results from this book:

➢ **Begin studying long before your test date**. This provides you ample time to learn the different math concepts. The earlier you begin studying for the test, the sharper your skills will be. Do not procrastinate! Provide yourself with plenty of time to learn the concepts and feel comfortable that you understand them when your test date arrives.

➢ **Practice consistently**. Study HiSET Math concepts at least 20 to 30 minutes a day. Remember, slow and steady wins the race, which can be applied to preparing for the HiSET Math test. Instead of cramming to tackle everything at once, be patient and learn the math topics in short bursts.

➢ Whenever you get a math problem wrong, **mark it off, and review it later** to make sure you understand the concept.

➢ Start each session by **looking over the previous material.**

➢ Once you've reviewed the book's exercises, **take a practice test at the back of the book** to gauge your level of readiness. Then, review your results. Read detailed answers and solutions for each question you missed.

➢ **Take another practice test** to get an idea of how ready you are to take the actual exam. Taking the practice tests will give you the confidence you need on test day. Simulate the HiSET testing environment by sitting in a quiet room free from distraction. Make sure to clock yourself with a timer.

How to Study for the HiSET Math Test

Studying for the HiSET Math test can be a really daunting and boring task. What's the best way to go about it? Is there a certain study method that works better than others? Well, studying for the HiSET Math can be done effectively. The following six-step program has been designed to make preparing for the HiSET Math test more efficient and less overwhelming.

Step **1** - Create a study plan
Step **2** - Choose your study resources
Step **3** - Review, Learn, Practice
Step **4** - Learn and practice test-taking strategies
Step **5** - Learn the HiSET Test format and take practice tests
Step **6** - Analyze your performance

STEP 1: Create a Study Plan

It's always easier to get things done when you have a plan. Creating a study plan for the HiSET Math test can help you to stay on track with your studies. It's important to sit down and prepare a study plan with what works with your life, work, and any other obligations you may have. Devote enough time each day to studying. It's also a great  idea to break down each section of the exam into blocks and study one concept at a time.

It's important to understand that there is no "right" way to create a study plan. Your study plan will be personalized based on your specific needs and learning style.

Follow these guidelines to create an effective study plan for your HiSET Math test:

★ **Analyze your learning style and study habits** – Everyone has a different learning style. It is essential to embrace your individuality and the unique way you learn. Think about what works and what doesn't work for you. Do you prefer HiSET Math prep books or a combination of textbooks and video lessons? Does it work better for you if you study every night for thirty minutes or is it more effective to study in the morning before going to work?

★ **Evaluate your schedule** – Review your current schedule and find out how much time you can consistently devote to HiSET Math study.

★ **Develop a schedule** – Now it's time to add your study schedule to your calendar like any other obligation. Schedule time for study, practice, and review. Plan out which topic you will study on which day to ensure that you're devoting enough time to each concept. Develop a study plan that is mindful, realistic, and flexible.

★ **Stick to your schedule** – A study plan is only effective when it is followed consistently. You should try to develop a study plan that you can follow for the length of your study program.

★ **Evaluate your study plan and adjust as needed** – Sometimes you need to adjust your plan when you have new commitments. Check in with yourself regularly to make sure that you're not falling behind in your study plan. Remember, the most important thing is sticking to your plan. Your study plan is all about helping you be more productive. If you find that your study plan is not as effective as you want, don't get discouraged. It's okay to make changes as you figure out what works best for you.

STEP 2: Choose Your Study Resources

There are numerous textbooks and online resources available for the HiSET Math test, and it may not be clear where to begin. Don't worry! This exercise book reviews all HiSET Math concepts and topics. In addition to the book content, you can also use Effortless Math's online resources. (video lessons, worksheets, formulas, etc.) On each page, there is a link (and a QR code)  to an online webpage which provides a comprehensive review of the topic, step-by-step instruction, video tutorial, and numerous examples and exercises to help you fully understand the concept.

Simply visit <u>EffortlessMath.com/HiSET</u> to find your online HiSET Math resources.

STEP 3: Review, Learn, Practice

This HiSET Math exercise book breaks down each subject into specific skills or content areas. For instance, the percent concept is separated into different topics—percent calculation, percent increase and decrease, percent problems, etc. Use this book to help you go over all key math concepts and topics on the HiSET Math test.

As you review each topic, take notes or highlight the concepts you would like to go over again in the future. If you're unfamiliar with a topic or something is difficult for you, use the link (or the QR code) at the top of the page to find the webpage that provides more instruction about that topic. For each math topic, plenty of instructions, step-by-step guides, and examples are provided to ensure you get a good grasp of the material.

Quickly review the topics you do understand to get a brush-up of the material. Be sure to do the practice questions provided at the end of every chapter to measure your understanding of the concepts.

STEP 4: Learn and Practice Test-taking Strategies

In the following sections, you will find important test-taking strategies and tips that can help you earn extra points. You'll learn how to think strategically and when to guess if you don't know the answer to a question. Using HiSET Math test-taking strategies and tips can help you raise your score and do well on the test. Apply test taking strategies on the practice tests to help you boost your confidence.

STEP 5: Learn the HiSET Test Format and Take Practice Tests

The HiSET *Test Review* section provides information about the structure of the HiSET test. Read this section to learn more about the HiSET test structure, different test sections, the number of questions in each section, and the section time limits. When you have a prior understanding of the test format and different types of HiSET Math questions,  you'll feel more confident when you take the actual exam.

Once you have read through the instructions and lessons and feel like you are ready to go – take advantage of both of the full-length HiSET Math practice tests available in this exercise book. Use the practice tests to sharpen your skills and build confidence.

The HiSET Math practice tests offered at the end of the book are formatted similarly to the actual HiSET Math test. When you take each practice test, try to simulate actual testing conditions. To take the practice tests, sit in a quiet space, time yourself, and work through as many of the questions as time allows. The practice tests are followed by detailed answer explanations to help you find your weak areas, learn from your mistakes, and raise your HiSET Math score.

STEP 6: Analyze Your Performance

After taking the practice tests, look over the answer keys and explanations to learn which questions you answered correctly and which you did not. Never be discouraged if you make a few mistakes. See them as a learning opportunity. This will highlight your strengths and weaknesses.

You can use the results to determine if you need additional practice or if you are ready to take the actual HiSET Math test.

Looking for more?

Visit EffortlessMath.com/HiSET to find hundreds of HiSET Math worksheets, video tutorials, practice tests, HiSET Math formulas, and much more.

Or scan this QR code.

No Registration Required.

HiSET Test Review

The High School Equivalency Test (HiSET), commonly known as HiSET, is a standardized test and was released in the year 2014. This test was created by the ITP (Iowa Testing Programs) and ETS (Educational Testing Service). The HiSET is equal to the HiSET test. Currently, there are twelve states that offer the HiSET®: California, Iowa, Louisiana, Maine, Massachusetts, Missouri, Montana, Nevada, New Hampshire, New Jersey, Tennessee, and Wyoming.

HiSET test takers can choose to take the test using a computer, or with pencil and paper.

The HiSET is made up of five distinct sections:

- Social Studies,
- Language Arts Reading
- Language Arts Writing
- Science
- Mathematics

The HiSET Mathematics test is a 90-minute, single-section test that covers basic mathematics topics, quantitative problem-solving and algebraic questions. There are approximately 50-55 Multiple-choice questions on Mathematics section. Calculator is allowed in the Math section.

HiSET Math Test-Taking Strategies

Here are some test-taking strategies that you can use to maximize your performance and results on the HiSET Math test.

#1 : USE THIS APPROACH TO ANSWER EVERY HiSET MATH QUESTION

- Review the question to identify keywords and important information.
- Translate the keywords into math operations so you can solve the problem.
- Review the answer choices. What are the differences between answer choices?
- Draw or label a diagram if needed.
- Try to find patterns.
- Find the right method to answer the question. Use straightforward math, plug in numbers, or test the answer choices (backsolving).
- Double-check your work.

#2 : USE EDUCATED GUESSING

This approach is applicable to the problems you understand to some degree but cannot solve using straightforward math. In such cases, try to filter out as many answer choices as possible before picking an answer. In cases where you don't have a clue about what a certain problem entails, don't waste any time trying to eliminate answer choices. Just choose one randomly before moving onto the next question.

As you can ascertain, direct solutions are the most optimal approach. Carefully read through the question, determine what the solution is using the math you have learned before, then coordinate the answer with one of the choices available to you. Are you stumped? Make your best guess, then move on.

Don't leave any fields empty! Even if you're unable to work out a problem, strive to answer it. Take a guess if you have to. You will not lose points by getting an answer wrong, though you may gain a point by getting it correct!

#3 : BALLPARK

A ballpark answer is a rough approximation. When we become overwhelmed by calculations and figures, we end up making silly mistakes. A decimal that is moved by one unit can change an answer from right to wrong, regardless of the number of steps that you went through to get it. That's where ballparking can play a big part.

If you think you know what the correct answer may be (even if it's just a ballpark answer), you'll usually have the ability to eliminate a couple of choices. While answer choices are usually based on the average student error and/or values that are closely tied, you will still be able to weed out choices that are way far afield. Try to find answers that aren't in the proverbial ballpark when you're looking for a wrong answer on a multiple-choice question. This is an optimal approach to eliminating answers to a problem.

#4 : BACKSOLVING

All questions on the HiSET Math test will be in multiple-choice format. Many test-takers prefer multiple-choice questions, as at least the answer is right there. You'll typically have four answers to pick from. You simply need to figure out which one is correct. Usually, the best way to go about doing so is "backsolving."

As mentioned earlier, direct solutions are the most optimal approach to answering a question. Carefully read through a problem, calculate a solution, then correspond the answer with one of the choices displayed in front of you. If you can't calculate a solution, your next best approach involves "backsolving."

When backsolving a problem, contrast one of your answer options against the problem you are asked, then see which of them is most relevant. More often than not, answer choices are listed in ascending or descending order. In such cases, try out the choices B or C. If it's not correct, you can go either down or up from there.

#5 : PLUGGING IN NUMBERS

"Plugging in numbers" is a strategy that can be applied to a wide range of different math problems on the HiSET Math test. This approach is typically used to simplify a challenging question so that it is more understandable. By using the strategy carefully, you can find the answer without too much trouble.

The concept is fairly straightforward–replace unknown variables in a problem with certain values. When selecting a number, consider the following:

- Choose a number that's basic (just not too basic). Generally, you should avoid choosing 1 (or even 0). A decent choice is 2.

- Try not to choose a number that is displayed in the problem.

- Make sure you keep your numbers different if you need to choose at least two of them.

- More often than not, choosing numbers merely lets you filter out some of your answer choices. As such, don't just go with the first choice that gives you the right answer.

- If several answers seem correct, then you'll need to choose another value and try again. This time, though, you'll just need to check choices that haven't been eliminated yet.

- If your question contains fractions, then a potential right answer may involve either an LCD (least common denominator) or an LCD multiple.

- 100 is the number you should choose when you are dealing with problems involving percentages.

HiSET Math – Test Day Tips

After practicing and reviewing all the math concepts you've been taught, and taking some HiSET mathematics practice tests, you'll be prepared for test day. Consider the following tips to be extra-ready come test time.

Before Your Test

What to do the night before:

- **Relax!** One day before your test, study lightly or skip studying altogether. You shouldn't attempt to learn something new, either. There are plenty of reasons why studying the evening before a big test can work against you. Put it this way–a marathoner wouldn't go out for a sprint before the day of a big race. Mental marathoners–such as yourself–should not study for any more than one hour 24 hours before a HiSET test. That's because your brain requires some rest to be at its best. The night before your exam, spend some time with family or friends, or read a book.

- **Avoid bright screens** - You'll have to get some good shuteye the night before your test. Bright screens (such as the ones coming from your laptop, TV, or mobile device) should be avoided altogether. Staring at such a screen will keep your brain up, making it hard to drift asleep at a reasonable hour.

- **Make sure your dinner is healthy** - The meal that you have for dinner should be nutritious. Be sure to drink plenty of water as well. Load up on your complex carbohydrates, much like a marathon runner would do. Pasta, rice, and potatoes are ideal options here, as are vegetables and protein sources.

- **Get your bag ready for test day** - The night prior to your test, pack your bag with your stationery, admissions pass, ID, and any other gear that you need. Keep the bag right by your front door.

- **Make plans to reach the testing site** - Before going to sleep, ensure that you understand precisely how you will arrive at the site of the test. If parking is something you'll have to find first, plan for it. If you're dependent on public transit, then review the schedule. You should also make sure that the train/bus/subway/streetcar you use will be running. Find out about road closures as well. If a parent or friend is accompanying you, ensure that they understand what steps they have to take as well.

The Day of the Test

■ **Get up reasonably early, but not too early.**

■ **Have breakfast** - Breakfast improves your concentration, memory, and mood. As such, make sure the breakfast that you eat in the morning is healthy. The last thing you want to be is distracted by a grumbling tummy. If it's not your own stomach making those noises, another test taker close to you might be instead. Prevent discomfort or embarrassment by consuming a healthy breakfast. Bring a snack with you if you think you'll need it.

■ **Follow your daily routine** - Do you watch Good Morning America each morning while getting ready for the day? Don't break your usual habits on the day of the test. Likewise, if coffee isn't something you drink in the morning, then don't take up the habit hours before your test. Routine consistency lets you concentrate on the main objective—doing the best you can on your test.

■ **Wear layers** - Dress yourself up in comfortable layers. You should be ready for any kind of internal temperature. If it gets too warm during the test, take a layer off.

■ **Get there on time** - The last thing you want to do is get to the test site late. Rather, you should be there 45 minutes prior to the start of the test. Upon your arrival, try not to hang out with anybody who is nervous. Any anxious energy they exhibit shouldn't influence you.

■ **Leave the books at home** - No books should be brought to the test site. If you start developing anxiety before the test, books could encourage you to do some last-minute studying, which will only hinder you. Keep the books far away—better yet, leave them at home.

■ **Make your voice heard** - If something is off, speak to a proctor. If medical attention is needed or if you'll require anything, consult the proctor prior to the start of the test. Any doubts you have should be clarified. You should be entering the test site with a state of mind that is completely clear.

- **Have faith in yourself** - When you feel confident, you will be able to perform at your best. When you are waiting for the test to begin, envision yourself receiving an outstanding result. Try to see yourself as someone who knows all the answers, no matter what the questions are. A lot of athletes tend to use this technique–particularly before a big competition. Your expectations will be reflected by your performance.

During your test

- **Be calm and breathe deeply** - You need to relax before the test, and some deep breathing will go a long way to help you do that. Be confident and calm. You got this. Everybody feels a little stressed out just before an evaluation of any kind is set to begin. Learn some effective breathing exercises. Spend a minute meditating before the test starts. Filter out any negative thoughts you have. Exhibit confidence when having such thoughts.

- **Concentrate on the test** - Refrain from comparing yourself to anyone else. You shouldn't be distracted by the people near you or random noise. Concentrate exclusively on the test. If you find yourself irritated by surrounding noises, earplugs can be used to block sounds off close to you. Don't forget–the test is going to last several hours if you're taking more than one subject of the test. Some of that time will be dedicated to brief sections. Concentrate on the specific section you are working on during a particular moment. Do not let your mind wander off to upcoming or previous sections.

- **Skip challenging questions** - Optimize your time when taking the test. Lingering on a single question for too long will work against you. If you don't know what the answer is to a certain question, use your best guess, and mark the question so you can review it later on. There is no need to spend time attempting to solve something you aren't sure about. That time would be better served handling the questions you can actually answer well. You will not be penalized for getting the wrong answer on a test like this.

- **Try to answer each question individually** - Focus only on the question you are working on. Use one of the test-taking strategies to solve the problem. If you aren't able to come up with an answer, don't get frustrated. Simply skip that question, then move onto the next one.

- **Don't forget to breathe!** Whenever you notice your mind wandering, your stress levels boosting, or frustration brewing, take a thirty-second break. Shut your eyes, drop your pencil, breathe deeply, and let your shoulders relax. You will end up being more productive when you allow yourself to relax for a moment.

- **Review your answer.** If you still have time at the end of the test, don't waste it. Go back and check over your answers. It is worth going through the test from start to finish to ensure that you didn't make a sloppy mistake somewhere.

- **Optimize your breaks** - When break time comes, use the restroom, have a snack, and reactivate your energy for the subsequent section. Doing some stretches can help stimulate your blood flow.

After your test

- **Take it easy** - You will need to set some time aside to relax and decompress once the test has concluded. There is no need to stress yourself out about what you could've said, or what you may have done wrong. At this point, there's nothing you can do about it. Your energy and time would be better spent on something that will bring you happiness for the remainder of your day.

- **Redoing the test** - Did you pass the test? Congratulations! Your hard work paid off!

  If you have failed your test, though, don't worry! The test can be retaken. In such cases, you will need to follow the retake policy. You also need to re-register to take the exam again.

Contents

Chapter 1: Fractions and Mixed Numbers

Math Topics that you'll learn in this Chapter:

- ✓ Simplifying Fractions
- ✓ Adding and Subtracting Fractions
- ✓ Multiplying and Dividing Fractions
- ✓ Adding Mixed Numbers
- ✓ Subtracting Mixed Numbers
- ✓ Multiplying Mixed Numbers
- ✓ Dividing Mixed Numbers

Simplifying Fractions

✎ *Simplify each fraction to its lowest terms.*

1) $\dfrac{9}{18} =$

2) $\dfrac{8}{10} =$

3) $\dfrac{6}{8} =$

4) $\dfrac{5}{20} =$

5) $\dfrac{18}{24} =$

6) $\dfrac{6}{9} =$

7) $\dfrac{12}{15} =$

8) $\dfrac{4}{16} =$

9) $\dfrac{18}{36} =$

10) $\dfrac{6}{42} =$

11) $\dfrac{13}{39} =$

12) $\dfrac{21}{28} =$

13) $\dfrac{63}{77} =$

14) $\dfrac{36}{40} =$

15) $\dfrac{21}{63} =$

16) $\dfrac{30}{84} =$

17) $\dfrac{50}{125} =$

18) $\dfrac{72}{108} =$

19) $\dfrac{49}{112} =$

20) $\dfrac{240}{320} =$

21) $\dfrac{120}{150} =$

✎ *Solve each problem.*

22) Which of the following fractions equal to $\dfrac{4}{5}$? _____

   A. $\dfrac{64}{75}$ B. $\dfrac{92}{115}$ C. $\dfrac{60}{85}$ D. $\dfrac{160}{220}$

23) Which of the following fractions equal to $\dfrac{3}{7}$? _____

   A. $\dfrac{63}{147}$ B. $\dfrac{75}{182}$ C. $\dfrac{54}{140}$ D. $\dfrac{39}{98}$

24) Which of the following fractions equal to $\dfrac{2}{9}$? _____

   A. $\dfrac{84}{386}$ B. $\dfrac{52}{234}$ C. $\dfrac{96}{450}$ D. $\dfrac{112}{522}$

Adding and Subtracting Fractions

✍ *Find the sum.*

1) $\frac{1}{3} + \frac{2}{3} =$

2) $\frac{1}{2} + \frac{1}{3} =$

3) $\frac{2}{5} + \frac{1}{2} =$

4) $\frac{3}{7} + \frac{2}{3} =$

5) $\frac{3}{4} + \frac{2}{5} =$

6) $\frac{3}{5} + \frac{1}{5} =$

7) $\frac{5}{9} + \frac{1}{2} =$

8) $\frac{3}{5} + \frac{3}{8} =$

9) $\frac{5}{9} + \frac{3}{7} =$

10) $\frac{5}{11} + \frac{1}{4} =$

11) $\frac{3}{7} + \frac{1}{6} =$

12) $\frac{3}{14} + \frac{3}{4} =$

✍ *Find the difference.*

13) $\frac{1}{2} - \frac{1}{3} =$

14) $\frac{4}{5} - \frac{2}{3} =$

15) $\frac{2}{3} - \frac{1}{6} =$

16) $\frac{3}{5} - \frac{1}{2} =$

17) $\frac{8}{9} - \frac{2}{5} =$

18) $\frac{4}{7} - \frac{1}{9} =$

19) $\frac{2}{5} - \frac{1}{4} =$

20) $\frac{5}{8} - \frac{2}{6} =$

21) $\frac{4}{15} - \frac{1}{10} =$

22) $\frac{7}{20} - \frac{1}{5} =$

23) $\frac{3}{18} - \frac{1}{12} =$

24) $\frac{9}{24} - \frac{3}{16} =$

25) $\frac{3}{7} - \frac{2}{5} =$

26) $\frac{5}{9} - \frac{1}{6} =$

27) $\frac{2}{5} - \frac{1}{10} =$

28) $\frac{5}{12} - \frac{2}{9} =$

29) $\frac{2}{13} - \frac{3}{7} =$

30) $\frac{4}{11} - \frac{5}{8} =$

Multiplying and Dividing Fractions

✍ *Find the value of each expression in lowest terms.*

1) $\frac{1}{2} \times \frac{3}{4} =$

2) $\frac{3}{5} \times \frac{2}{3} =$

3) $\frac{1}{4} \times \frac{2}{5} =$

4) $\frac{1}{6} \times \frac{4}{5} =$

5) $\frac{1}{5} \times \frac{1}{4} =$

6) $\frac{2}{5} \times \frac{1}{2} =$

7) $\frac{7}{9} \times \frac{1}{3} =$

8) $\frac{5}{7} \times \frac{3}{8} =$

9) $\frac{8}{9} \times \frac{6}{7} =$

10) $\frac{5}{6} \times \frac{3}{5} =$

11) $\frac{3}{8} \times \frac{1}{9} =$

12) $\frac{1}{12} \times \frac{3}{7} =$

✍ *Find the value of each expression in lowest terms.*

13) $\frac{1}{2} \div \frac{1}{4} =$

14) $\frac{1}{3} \div \frac{1}{2} =$

15) $\frac{2}{5} \div \frac{1}{3} =$

16) $\frac{1}{4} \div \frac{2}{3} =$

17) $\frac{1}{5} \div \frac{3}{10} =$

18) $\frac{2}{7} \div \frac{1}{3} =$

19) $\frac{3}{5} \div \frac{5}{9} =$

20) $\frac{2}{23} \div \frac{2}{9} =$

21) $\frac{4}{13} \div \frac{1}{4} =$

22) $\frac{9}{14} \div \frac{3}{7} =$

23) $\frac{8}{15} \div \frac{2}{5} =$

24) $\frac{2}{9} \div \frac{7}{11} =$

25) $\frac{2}{5} \div \frac{3}{4} =$

26) $\frac{4}{11} \div \frac{2}{5} =$

27) $\frac{2}{15} \div \frac{5}{8} =$

28) $\frac{3}{10} \div \frac{2}{5} =$

29) $\frac{4}{5} \div \frac{3}{7} =$

30) $\frac{2}{11} \div \frac{3}{5} =$

Adding Mixed Numbers

✒️ *Solve and write the answer in lowest terms*

1) $1\frac{1}{5} + 2\frac{2}{5} =$

2) $1\frac{1}{2} + 4\frac{5}{6} =$

3) $2\frac{4}{5} + 2\frac{3}{10} =$

4) $3\frac{1}{6} + 2\frac{2}{5} =$

5) $1\frac{5}{6} + 1\frac{2}{5} =$

6) $3\frac{5}{7} + 1\frac{2}{9} =$

7) $3\frac{5}{8} + 2\frac{1}{3} =$

8) $1\frac{6}{7} + 3\frac{2}{9} =$

9) $2\frac{5}{9} + 1\frac{1}{4} =$

10) $3\frac{7}{9} + 2\frac{5}{6} =$

11) $2\frac{1}{10} + 2\frac{2}{5} =$

12) $1\frac{3}{10} + 3\frac{4}{5} =$

13) $3\frac{1}{12} + 2\frac{1}{3} =$

14) $5\frac{1}{11} + 1\frac{1}{2} =$

15) $3\frac{1}{21} + 2\frac{2}{3} =$

16) $4\frac{1}{24} + 1\frac{5}{8} =$

17) $2\frac{1}{25} + 3\frac{3}{5} =$

18) $3\frac{1}{15} + 2\frac{2}{10} =$

19) $5\frac{6}{7} + 2\frac{1}{3} =$

20) $2\frac{1}{8} + 3\frac{3}{4} =$

21) $2\frac{5}{7} + 2\frac{2}{21} =$

22) $4\frac{1}{6} + 1\frac{4}{5} =$

23) $2\frac{1}{7} + 2\frac{3}{8} =$

24) $3\frac{1}{4} + 2\frac{2}{3} =$

25) $1\frac{1}{13} + 2\frac{3}{4} =$

26) $3\frac{2}{35} + 2\frac{5}{7} =$

Subtracting Mixed Numbers

✍ *Solve and write the answer in lowest terms.*

1) $5\frac{2}{9} - 2\frac{1}{9} =$

2) $6\frac{2}{7} - 2\frac{1}{3} =$

3) $5\frac{3}{8} - 2\frac{3}{4} =$

4) $7\frac{2}{5} - 3\frac{1}{10} =$

5) $9\frac{5}{7} - 7\frac{4}{21} =$

6) $11\frac{7}{12} - 9\frac{5}{6} =$

7) $9\frac{5}{9} - 8\frac{1}{8} =$

8) $13\frac{7}{9} - 11\frac{3}{7} =$

9) $8\frac{7}{12} - 7\frac{3}{8} =$

10) $11\frac{5}{9} - 9\frac{1}{4} =$

11) $6\frac{5}{6} - 2\frac{2}{9} =$

12) $5\frac{7}{8} - 4\frac{1}{3} =$

13) $9\frac{5}{8} - 8\frac{1}{2} =$

14) $4\frac{9}{16} - 2\frac{1}{4} =$

15) $3\frac{2}{3} - 1\frac{2}{15} =$

16) $5\frac{1}{2} - 4\frac{2}{17} =$

17) $5\frac{6}{7} - 2\frac{1}{3} =$

18) $3\frac{3}{7} - 2\frac{2}{21} =$

19) $7\frac{3}{10} - 5\frac{2}{15} =$

20) $4\frac{5}{6} - 2\frac{2}{9} =$

21) $6\frac{3}{7} - 2\frac{2}{9} =$

22) $7\frac{4}{5} - 6\frac{3}{7} =$

23) $12\frac{3}{7} - 8\frac{1}{3} =$

24) $5\frac{4}{9} - 2\frac{5}{6} =$

25) $10\frac{1}{28} - 7\frac{3}{4} =$

26) $11\frac{5}{12} - 7\frac{5}{48} =$

Multiplying Mixed Numbers

✎ *Solve and write the answer in lowest terms*

1) $1\frac{1}{6} \times 1\frac{3}{7} =$

2) $5\frac{1}{6} \times 2\frac{1}{4} =$

3) $3\frac{3}{7} \times 1\frac{2}{9} =$

4) $3\frac{3}{8} \times 3\frac{1}{6} =$

5) $1\frac{1}{2} \times 5\frac{2}{3} =$

6) $3\frac{1}{2} \times 6\frac{2}{3} =$

7) $9\frac{1}{2} \times 2\frac{1}{6} =$

8) $2\frac{5}{8} \times 8\frac{3}{5} =$

9) $3\frac{4}{5} \times 4\frac{2}{3} =$

10) $5\frac{1}{3} \times 2\frac{2}{7} =$

11) $6\frac{1}{3} \times 3\frac{3}{4} =$

12) $7\frac{2}{3} \times 1\frac{8}{9} =$

13) $8\frac{1}{2} \times 2\frac{1}{6} =$

14) $4\frac{1}{5} \times 8\frac{2}{3} =$

15) $3\frac{1}{8} \times 5\frac{2}{3} =$

16) $2\frac{2}{7} \times 6\frac{2}{5} =$

17) $2\frac{3}{8} \times 7\frac{2}{3} =$

18) $1\frac{7}{8} \times 8\frac{2}{3} =$

19) $9\frac{1}{2} \times 3\frac{1}{5} =$

20) $2\frac{5}{8} \times 4\frac{1}{3} =$

21) $6\frac{1}{3} \times 3\frac{2}{5} =$

22) $5\frac{3}{4} \times 2\frac{2}{7} =$

23) $8\frac{1}{6} \times 2\frac{2}{7} =$

24) $4\frac{1}{6} \times 7\frac{1}{5} =$

25) $2\frac{1}{5} \times 2\frac{5}{8} =$

26) $6\frac{2}{3} \times 4\frac{3}{5} =$

Dividing Mixed Numbers

✎ *Solve and write the answer in lowest terms*

1) $6\frac{1}{2} \div 4\frac{2}{5} =$

2) $1\frac{3}{8} \div 1\frac{1}{4} =$

3) $6\frac{2}{5} \div 2\frac{4}{5} =$

4) $7\frac{1}{3} \div 6\frac{3}{4} =$

5) $7\frac{2}{5} \div 3\frac{3}{4} =$

6) $2\frac{4}{5} \div 3\frac{2}{3} =$

7) $8\frac{3}{5} \div 4\frac{3}{4} =$

8) $6\frac{3}{4} \div 2\frac{2}{9} =$

9) $5\frac{2}{7} \div 2\frac{2}{9} =$

10) $2\frac{2}{5} \div 3\frac{3}{5} =$

11) $4\frac{3}{7} \div 1\frac{7}{8} =$

12) $2\frac{5}{7} \div 2\frac{4}{5} =$

13) $8\frac{3}{5} \div 6\frac{1}{5} =$

14) $2\frac{5}{8} \div 1\frac{8}{9} =$

15) $5\frac{6}{7} \div 2\frac{3}{4} =$

16) $1\frac{3}{5} \div 2\frac{3}{8} =$

17) $5\frac{3}{4} \div 3\frac{2}{5} =$

18) $2\frac{3}{4} \div 3\frac{1}{5} =$

19) $3\frac{2}{3} \div 1\frac{2}{5} =$

20) $4\frac{1}{4} \div 2\frac{2}{3} =$

21) $3\frac{5}{6} \div 2\frac{4}{5} =$

22) $2\frac{1}{8} \div 1\frac{3}{4} =$

23) $5\frac{1}{2} \div 4\frac{2}{5} =$

24) $6\frac{3}{7} \div 2\frac{1}{7} =$

25) $3\frac{3}{6} \div 1\frac{5}{7} =$

26) $4\frac{4}{9} \div 4\frac{2}{3} =$

Answers – Chapter 1

Simplifying Fractions

1) $\dfrac{1}{2}$

2) $\dfrac{4}{5}$

3) $\dfrac{3}{4}$

4) $\dfrac{1}{4}$

5) $\dfrac{3}{4}$

6) $\dfrac{2}{3}$

7) $\dfrac{4}{5}$

8) $\dfrac{1}{4}$

9) $\dfrac{1}{2}$

10) $\dfrac{1}{7}$

11) $\dfrac{1}{3}$

12) $\dfrac{3}{4}$

13) $\dfrac{9}{11}$

14) $\dfrac{9}{10}$

15) $\dfrac{1}{3}$

16) $\dfrac{5}{14}$

17) $\dfrac{2}{5}$

18) $\dfrac{2}{3}$

19) $\dfrac{7}{16}$

20) $\dfrac{3}{4}$

21) $\dfrac{4}{5}$

22) B

23) A

24) B

Adding and Subtracting Fractions

1) $\dfrac{3}{3} = 1$

2) $\dfrac{5}{6}$

3) $\dfrac{9}{10}$

4) $\dfrac{23}{21}$

5) $\dfrac{23}{20}$

6) $\dfrac{4}{5}$

7) $\dfrac{19}{18}$

8) $\dfrac{39}{40}$

9) $\dfrac{62}{63}$

10) $\dfrac{31}{44}$

11) $\dfrac{25}{42}$

12) $\dfrac{27}{28}$

13) $\dfrac{1}{6}$

14) $\dfrac{2}{15}$

15) $\dfrac{1}{2}$

16) $\dfrac{1}{10}$

17) $\dfrac{22}{45}$

18) $\dfrac{29}{63}$

19) $\dfrac{3}{20}$

20) $\dfrac{7}{24}$

21) $\dfrac{1}{6}$

22) $\dfrac{3}{20}$

23) $\dfrac{1}{12}$

24) $\dfrac{3}{16}$

25) $\dfrac{1}{35}$

26) $\dfrac{7}{18}$

27) $\dfrac{3}{10}$

28) $\dfrac{7}{36}$

29) $-\dfrac{25}{91}$

30) $-\dfrac{23}{88}$

Multiplying and Dividing Fractions

1) $\dfrac{3}{8}$

2) $\dfrac{2}{5}$

3) $\dfrac{1}{10}$

4) $\dfrac{2}{15}$

5) $\dfrac{1}{20}$

6) $\dfrac{1}{5}$

7) $\dfrac{7}{27}$

8) $\dfrac{15}{56}$

9) $\dfrac{16}{21}$

10) $\dfrac{1}{2}$

11) $\dfrac{1}{24}$

12) $\dfrac{1}{28}$

13) 2

14) $\dfrac{2}{3}$

15) $\dfrac{6}{5}$

16) $\dfrac{3}{8}$

17) $\dfrac{2}{3}$

18) $\dfrac{6}{7}$

19) $\dfrac{27}{25}$

20) $\dfrac{9}{23}$

21) $\dfrac{16}{13}$

22) $\dfrac{3}{2}$

23) $\dfrac{4}{3}$

24) $\dfrac{22}{63}$

25) $\dfrac{8}{15}$

26) $\dfrac{10}{11}$

27) $\dfrac{16}{75}$

28) $\dfrac{3}{4}$

29) $\dfrac{28}{15}$

30) $\dfrac{10}{33}$

Adding Mixed Numbers

1) $3\dfrac{3}{5}$

2) $6\dfrac{1}{3}$

3) $5\dfrac{1}{10}$

4) $5\dfrac{17}{30}$

5) $3\dfrac{7}{30}$

6) $4\dfrac{59}{63}$

7) $5\dfrac{23}{24}$

8) $5\dfrac{5}{63}$

9) $3\dfrac{29}{36}$

10) $6\dfrac{11}{18}$

11) $4\dfrac{1}{2}$

12) $5\dfrac{1}{10}$

13) $5\dfrac{5}{12}$

14) $6\dfrac{13}{22}$

15) $5\dfrac{5}{7}$

16) $5\dfrac{2}{3}$

17) $5\dfrac{16}{25}$

18) $5\dfrac{4}{15}$

19) $8\dfrac{4}{21}$

20) $5\dfrac{7}{8}$

21) $4\dfrac{17}{21}$

22) $5\dfrac{29}{30}$

23) $4\dfrac{29}{56}$

24) $5\dfrac{11}{12}$

25) $3\dfrac{43}{52}$

26) $5\dfrac{27}{35}$

Subtracting Mixed Numbers

1) $3\dfrac{1}{9}$

2) $3\dfrac{20}{21}$

3) $2\dfrac{5}{8}$

4) $4\dfrac{3}{10}$

5) $2\dfrac{11}{21}$

6) $1\dfrac{3}{4}$

7) $1\dfrac{31}{72}$

8) $2\dfrac{22}{63}$

9) $1\dfrac{5}{24}$

10) $2\dfrac{11}{36}$

11) $4\dfrac{11}{18}$

12) $1\dfrac{13}{24}$

13) $1\dfrac{1}{8}$

14) $2\dfrac{5}{16}$

15) $2\dfrac{8}{15}$

16) $1\dfrac{13}{34}$

17) $3\dfrac{11}{21}$

18) $1\dfrac{1}{3}$

19) $2\dfrac{1}{6}$

20) $2\dfrac{11}{18}$

21) $4\dfrac{13}{63}$

22) $1\dfrac{13}{35}$

23) $4\dfrac{2}{21}$

24) $2\dfrac{11}{18}$

25) $2\dfrac{2}{7}$

26) $4\dfrac{5}{16}$

Multiplying Mixed Numbers

1) $1\frac{2}{3}$

2) $11\frac{5}{8}$

3) $4\frac{4}{21}$

4) $10\frac{11}{16}$

5) $8\frac{1}{2}$

6) $23\frac{1}{3}$

7) $20\frac{7}{12}$

8) $22\frac{23}{40}$

9) $17\frac{11}{15}$

10) $12\frac{4}{21}$

11) $23\frac{3}{4}$

12) $14\frac{13}{27}$

13) $18\frac{5}{12}$

14) $36\frac{2}{5}$

15) $17\frac{17}{24}$

16) $14\frac{22}{35}$

17) $18\frac{5}{24}$

18) $16\frac{1}{4}$

19) $30\frac{2}{5}$

20) $11\frac{3}{8}$

21) $21\frac{8}{15}$

22) $13\frac{1}{7}$

23) $18\frac{2}{3}$

24) 30

25) $5\frac{31}{40}$

26) $30\frac{2}{3}$

Dividing Mixed Numbers

1) $1\frac{21}{44}$

2) $1\frac{1}{10}$

3) $2\frac{2}{7}$

4) $1\frac{7}{81}$

5) $1\frac{73}{75}$

6) $\frac{42}{55}$

7) $1\frac{77}{95}$

8) $3\frac{3}{80}$

9) $2\frac{53}{140}$

10) $\frac{2}{3}$

11) $2\frac{38}{105}$

12) $\frac{95}{98}$

13) $1\frac{12}{31}$

14) $1\frac{53}{136}$

15) $2\frac{10}{77}$

16) $\frac{64}{95}$

17) $1\frac{47}{68}$

18) $\frac{55}{64}$

19) $2\frac{13}{21}$

20) $1\frac{19}{32}$

21) $1\frac{31}{84}$

22) $1\frac{3}{14}$

23) $1\frac{1}{4}$

24) 3

25) $2\frac{1}{24}$

26) $\frac{20}{21}$

Effortless Math Education

Chapter 2: Decimal

Math Topics that you'll learn in this Chapter:

- ✓ Comparing Decimals
- ✓ Rounding Decimals
- ✓ Adding and Subtracting Decimals
- ✓ Multiplying and Dividing Decimals

13

Comparing Decimals

✍ *Write the correct comparison symbol (>, < or =).*

1) 0.50 ☐ 0.050

2) 0.025 ☐ 0.25

3) 2.060 ☐ 2.07

4) 1.75 ☐ 1.07

5) 4.04 ☐ 0.440

6) 3.05 ☐ 3.5

7) 5.05 ☐ 5.050

8) 1.02 ☐ 1.1

9) 2.45 ☐ 2.125

10) 0.932 ☐ 0.0932

11) 3.15 ☐ 3.150

12) 0.718 ☐ 0.89

13) 7.060 ☐ 7.60

14) 3.59 ☐ 3.129

15) 4.33 ☐ 4.319

16) 2.25 ☐ 2.250

17) 1.95 ☐ 1.095

18) 8.051 ☐ 8.50

19) 1.022 ☐ 1.020

20) 3.77 ☐ 3.770

Rounding Decimals

✎ **Round each decimal to the nearest whole number.**

1) 23.18   3) 14.45   5) 3.95

2) 8.6   4) 7.5   6) 56.7

✎ **Round each decimal to the nearest tenth.**

7) 22.652   9) 47.847   11) 16.184

8) 30.342   10) 82.88   12) 71.79

✎ **Round each decimal to the nearest hundredth.**

13) 5.439   15) 26.1855 17) 91.448

14) 12.907 16) 48.623   18) 29.354

✎ **Round each decimal to the nearest thousandth.**

19) 14.67374 21) 78.7191   23) 10.0678

20) 7.54647   22) 70.2732   24) 46.54765

Adding and Subtracting Decimals

 Add and subtract decimals.

1)
$$
\begin{array}{r}
31.13 \\
- \ 11.45 \\
\hline
\end{array}
$$

4)
$$
\begin{array}{r}
56.67 \\
- \ 44.39 \\
\hline
\end{array}
$$

7)
$$
\begin{array}{r}
66.24 \\
- \ 23.11 \\
\hline
\end{array}
$$

2)
$$
\begin{array}{r}
35.25 \\
+ \ 24.47 \\
\hline
\end{array}
$$

5)
$$
\begin{array}{r}
71.47 \\
+ \ 16.25 \\
\hline
\end{array}
$$

8)
$$
\begin{array}{r}
39.75 \\
+ \ 12.85 \\
\hline
\end{array}
$$

3)
$$
\begin{array}{r}
73.50 \\
+ \ 22.78 \\
\hline
\end{array}
$$

6)
$$
\begin{array}{r}
68.99 \\
- \ 53.61 \\
\hline
\end{array}
$$

9)
$$
\begin{array}{r}
229.25 \\
- \ 84.67 \\
\hline
\end{array}
$$

Find the missing number.

10) $\underline{} + 2.5 = 3.9$

11) $1.7 + \underline{} = 4.98$

12) $5.25 + \underline{} = 7$

13) $6.55 - \underline{} = 2.45$

14) $\underline{} - 3.98 = 5.32$

15) $\underline{} - 11.67 = 14.48$

16) $12.35 + \underline{} = 14.78$

17) $\underline{} - 23.89 = 13.90$

18) $\underline{} + 17.28 = 19.56$

19) $77.90 + \underline{} = 102.60$

Multiplying and Dividing Decimals

✍️ *Find the product.*

1) $0.5 \times 0.4 =$

2) $2.5 \times 0.2 =$

3) $1.25 \times 0.5 =$

4) $0.75 \times 0.2 =$

5) $1.92 \times 0.8 =$

6) $0.55 \times 0.4 =$

7) $3.24 \times 1.2 =$

8) $12.5 \times 4.2 =$

9) $22.6 \times 8.2 =$

10) $17.2 \times 4.5 =$

11) $25.1 \times 12.5 =$

12) $33.2 \times 2.2 =$

✍️ *Find the quotient.*

13) $1.67 \div 100 =$

14) $52.2 \div 1,000 =$

15) $4.2 \div 2 =$

16) $8.6 \div 0.5 =$

17) $12.6 \div 0.2 =$

18) $16.5 \div 5 =$

19) $13.25 \div 100 =$

20) $25.6 \div 0.4 =$

21) $28.24 \div 0.1 =$

22) $34.16 \div 0.25 =$

23) $44.28 \div 0.5 =$

24) $38.78 \div 0.02 =$

Answers – Chapter 2

Comparing Decimals

1) >
2) <
3) <
4) >
5) >
6) <
7) =

8) <
9) >
10) >
11) =
12) <
13) <
14) >

15) >
16) =
17) >
18) <
19) >
20) =

Rounding Decimals

1) 23
2) 9
3) 14
4) 8
5) 4
6) 57
7) 22.7
8) 30.3

9) 47.8
10) 82.9
11) 16.2
12) 71.8
13) 5.44
14) 12.91
15) 26.19
16) 48.62

17) 91.45
18) 29.35
19) 14.674
20) 7.546
21) 78.719
22) 70.273
23) 10.068
24) 46.548

Adding and Subtracting Decimals

1) 19.68
2) 59.72
3) 96.28
4) 12.28
5) 87.72
6) 15.38
7) 43.13

8) 52.60
9) 144.58
10) 1.4
11) 3.28
12) 1.75
13) 4.1
14) 9.3

15) 26.15
16) 2.43
17) 37.79
18) 2.28
19) 24.7

Multiplying and Dividing Decimals

1) 0.2
2) 0.5
3) 0.625
4) 0.15
5) 1.536
6) 0.22
7) 3.888
8) 52.5
9) 185.32

10) 77.4
11) 313.75
12) 73.04
13) 0.0167
14) 0.0522
15) 2.1
16) 17.2
17) 63
18) 3.3

19) 0.1325
20) 64
21) 282.4
22) 136.64
23) 88.56
24) 1,939

Chapter 3: Integers and Order of Operations

Math Topics that you'll learn in this Chapter:

- ✓ Adding and Subtracting Integers
- ✓ Multiplying and Dividing Integers
- ✓ Order of Operations
- ✓ Integers and Absolute Value

Adding and Subtracting Integers

✎ *Find each sum.*

1) $12 + (-5) =$

2) $(-14) + (-18) =$

3) $8 + (-28) =$

4) $43 + (-12) =$

5) $(-7) + (-11) + 4 =$

6) $37 + (-16) + 12 =$

7) $29 + (-21) + (-12) + 20 =$

8) $(-15) + (-25) + 18 + 25 =$

9) $30 + (-28) + (35 - 32) =$

10) $25 + (-15) + (44 - 17) =$

✎ *Find each difference.*

11) $(-12) - (-8) =$

12) $15 - (-20) =$

13) $(-11) - 25 =$

14) $30 - (-16) =$

15) $56 - (45 - 23) =$

16) $15 - (-4) - (-34) =$

17) $(24 + 14) - (-55) =$

18) $23 - 15 - (-3) =$

19) $49 - (15 + 12) - (-4) =$

20) $29 - (-17) - (-25) =$

21) $12 - (-8) - (-18) =$

22) $(15 - 28) - (-22) =$

23) $19 - 44 - (-14) =$

24) $67 - (57 + 19) - (-8) =$

25) $56 - (-12) + (-19) =$

26) $22 - (-44) + (-55) =$

Multiplying and Dividing Integers

✎ **Find each product.**

1) $(-7) \times (-8) =$

2) $(-4) \times 5 =$

3) $5 \times (-11) =$

4) $(-5) \times (-20) =$

5) $-(2) \times (-8) \times 3 =$

6) $(12 - 4) \times (-10) =$

7) $14 \times (-10) \times (-5) =$

8) $(18 + 12) \times (-8) =$

9) $9 \times (-15 + 6) \times 3 =$

10) $(-5) \times (-8) \times (-12) =$

✎ **Find each quotient.**

11) $16 \div (-4) =$

12) $(-25) \div (-5) =$

13) $(-40) \div (-8) =$

14) $64 \div (-8) =$

15) $(-49) \div 7 =$

16) $(-112) \div (-4) =$

17) $168 \div (-12) =$

18) $(-121) \div (-11) =$

19) $216 \div (-12) =$

20) $-(152) \div (8) =$

21) $(-152) \div (-8) =$

22) $-216 \div (-12) =$

23) $(-198) \div (-9) =$

24) $195 \div (-13) =$

25) $-(182) \div (-7) =$

26) $(126) \div (-14) =$

Order of Operations

✏ *Evaluate each expression.*

1) $5 + (4 \times 2) =$

2) $13 - (2 \times 5) =$

3) $(16 \times 2) + 18 =$

4) $(12 - 5) - (4 \times 3) =$

5) $25 + (14 \div 2) =$

6) $(18 \times 5) \div 5 =$

7) $(48 \div 2) \times (-4) =$

8) $(7 \times 5) + (25 - 12) =$

9) $64 + (3 \times 2) + 8 =$

10) $(20 \times 5) \div (4 + 1) =$

11) $(-9) + (12 \times 6) + 15 =$

12) $(7 \times 8) - (56 \div 4) =$

13) $(4 \times 8 \div 2) - (17 + 11) =$

14) $(18 + 8 - 15) \times 5 - 3 =$

15) $(25 - 12 + 45) \times (95 \div 5) =$

16) $28 + \left(15 - (32 \div 2)\right) =$

17) $(6 + 7 - 4 - 9) + (18 \div 2) =$

18) $(95 - 17) + (10 - 25 + 9) =$

19) $(18 \times 2) + (15 \times 5) - 12 =$

20) $12 + 8 - (42 \times 4) + 50 =$

Integers and Absolute Value

✎ *Write absolute value of each number.*

1) $|-7| =$

2) $|-11| =$

3) $|-9| =$

4) $|8| =$

5) $|4| =$

6) $|-18| =$

7) $|6| =$

8) $|0| =$

9) $|16| =$

10) $|-2| =$

11) $|-12|$

12) $|10| =$

13) $|3| =$

14) $|7| =$

15) $|-15| =$

16) $|-13| =$

17) $|19| =$

18) $|-12| =$

19) $|4| =$

20) $|-25| =$

✎ *Evaluate the value.*

21) $|-2| - \frac{|-10|}{2} =$

22) $8 - |2 - 14| - |-2| =$

23) $\frac{|-36|}{6} \times |-6| =$

24) $\frac{|5 \times -3|}{5} \times \frac{|-20|}{4} =$

25) $|2 \times -4| + \frac{|-40|}{5} =$

26) $\frac{|-28|}{4} \times \frac{|-55|}{11} =$

27) $|-12 + 4| \times \frac{|-4 \times 5|}{2}$

28) $\frac{|-10 \times 3|}{2} \times |-12| =$

Answers – Chapter 3

Adding and Subtracting Integers

1) 7
2) −32
3) −20
4) 31
5) −14
6) 33
7) 16
8) 3
9) 5

10) 37
11) −4
12) 35
13) −36
14) 46
15) 34
16) 53
17) 93
18) 11

19) 26
20) 71
21) 38
22) 9
23) −11
24) −1
25) 49
26) 11

Multiplying and Dividing Integers

1) 56
2) −20
3) −55
4) 100
5) 48
6) −80
7) 700
8) −240
9) −243

10) −480
11) −4
12) 5
13) 5
14) −8
15) −7
16) 28
17) −14
18) 11

19) −18
20) −19
21) 19
22) 18
23) 22
24) −15
25) 26
26) −9

Order of Operations

1) 13
2) 3
3) 50
4) −5
5) 32
6) 18
7) −96

8) 48
9) 78
10) 20
11) 78
12) 42
13) −12
14) 52

15) 1,102
16) 27
17) 9
18) 72
19) 99
20) −98

Effortless
Math
Education

Integers and Absolute Value

1) 7
2) 11
3) 9
4) 8
5) 4
6) 18
7) 6
8) 0
9) 16
10) 2

11) 12
12) 10
13) 3
14) 7
15) 15
16) 13
17) 19
18) 12
19) 4
20) 25

21) -3
22) -6
23) 36
24) 15
25) 16
26) 35
27) 80
28) 180

Effortless
Math
Education

Chapter 4: Ratios and Proportions

Math Topics that you'll learn in this Chapter:

- ✓ Simplifying Ratios
- ✓ Proportional Ratios
- ✓ Create Proportion
- ✓ Similarity and Ratios
- ✓ Simple Interest

Simplifying Ratios

✍ *Reduce each ratio.*

1) $12 : 8 =$ ___ : ___

2) $2 : 20 =$ ___ : ___

3) $3 : 36 =$ ___ : ___

4) $8 : 16 =$ ___ : ___

5) $6 : 100 =$ ___ : ___

6) $10 : 60 =$ ___ : ___

7) $21 : 49 =$ ___ : ___

8) $20 : 40 =$ ___ : ___

9) $10 : 50 =$ ___ : ___

10) $14 : 18 =$ ___ : ___

11) $45 : 27 =$ ___ : ___

12) $49 : 21 =$ ___ : ___

13) $100 : 10 =$ ___ : ___

14) $35 : 45 =$ ___ : ___

15) $8 : 20 =$ ___ : ___

16) $25 : 35 =$ ___ : ___

17) $21 : 27 =$ ___ : ___

18) $52 : 82 =$ ___ : ___

19) $12 : 36 =$ ___ : ___

20) $24 : 3 =$ ___ : ___

21) $15 : 30 =$ ___ : ___

22) $14 : 63 =$ ___ : ___

23) $68 : 80 =$ ___ : ___

24) $8 : 80 =$ ___ : ___

✍ *Write each ratio as a fraction in simplest form.*

25) $2 : 4 =$

26) $6 : 20 =$

27) $5 : 35 =$

28) $10 : 55 =$

29) $8 : 24 =$

30) $9 : 42 =$

31) $12 : 48 =$

32) $6 : 40 =$

33) $15 : 36 =$

34) $18 : 82 =$

35) $22 : 26 =$

36) $8 : 36 =$

37) $16 : 128 =$

38) $14 : 77 =$

39) $12 : 180 =$

40) $36 : 108 =$

41) $24 : 42 =$

42) $18 : 120 =$

43) $44 : 82 =$

44) $60 : 240 =$

45) $36 : 180 =$

Proportional Ratios

✏️ **Fill in the blanks; solve each proportion.**

1) $3 : 7 = \underline{\quad} : 49$

2) $1 : 2 = 20 : \underline{\quad}$

3) $1 : 5 = \underline{\quad} : 50$

4) $7 : 9 = 14 : \underline{\quad}$

5) $5 : 3 = 45 : \underline{\quad}$

6) $7 : 3 = \underline{\quad} : 18$

7) $10 : 1 = \underline{\quad} : 10$

8) $1 : 3 = \underline{\quad} : 27$

9) $8 : 1 = \underline{\quad} : 8$

10) $9 : 2 = \underline{\quad} : 14$

11) $3 : 12 = 12 : \underline{\quad}$

12) $6 : 4 = 24 : \underline{\quad}$

✏️ **State if each pair of ratios form a proportion.**

13) $\frac{3}{10}$ and $\frac{9}{30}$

14) $\frac{1}{2}$ and $\frac{16}{32}$

15) $\frac{5}{6}$ and $\frac{35}{42}$

16) $\frac{3}{7}$ and $\frac{27}{72}$

17) $\frac{2}{5}$ and $\frac{16}{45}$

18) $\frac{4}{9}$ and $\frac{40}{81}$

19) $\frac{6}{11}$ and $\frac{42}{77}$

20) $\frac{1}{6}$ and $\frac{8}{48}$

21) $\frac{6}{17}$ and $\frac{36}{85}$

22) $\frac{2}{7}$ and $\frac{24}{86}$

23) $\frac{12}{19}$ and $\frac{156}{247}$

24) $\frac{13}{21}$ and $\frac{182}{294}$

✏️ **Solve each proportion.**

25) $\frac{2}{5} = \frac{14}{x}, x = \underline{\quad}$

26) $\frac{1}{6} = \frac{7}{x}, x = \underline{\quad}$

27) $\frac{3}{5} = \frac{27}{x}, x = \underline{\quad}$

28) $\frac{1}{5} = \frac{x}{80}, x = \underline{\quad}$

29) $\frac{3}{7} = \frac{x}{63}, x = \underline{\quad}$

30) $\frac{1}{4} = \frac{13}{x}, x = \underline{\quad}$

31) $\frac{7}{9} = \frac{56}{x}, x = \underline{\quad}$

32) $\frac{6}{11} = \frac{42}{x}, x = \underline{\quad}$

33) $\frac{4}{7} = \frac{x}{77}, x = \underline{\quad}$

34) $\frac{5}{13} = \frac{x}{143}, x = \underline{\quad}$

35) $\frac{7}{19} = \frac{x}{209}, x = \underline{\quad}$

36) $\frac{3}{13} = \frac{x}{195}, x = \underline{\quad}$

Find more at bit.ly/37GHQxp

Create Proportion

✍ *State if each pair of ratios form a proportion.*

1) $\frac{3}{8}$ and $\frac{24}{50}$

2) $\frac{3}{11}$ and $\frac{6}{22}$

3) $\frac{4}{5}$ and $\frac{16}{20}$

4) $\frac{5}{11}$ and $\frac{12}{33}$

5) $\frac{5}{10}$ and $\frac{15}{30}$

6) $\frac{4}{13}$ and $\frac{8}{24}$

7) $\frac{6}{9}$ and $\frac{24}{36}$

8) $\frac{7}{12}$ and $\frac{14}{20}$

9) $\frac{3}{8}$ and $\frac{27}{72}$

10) $\frac{12}{20}$ and $\frac{36}{60}$

11) $\frac{11}{12}$ and $\frac{55}{60}$

12) $\frac{12}{15}$ and $\frac{24}{25}$

13) $\frac{15}{19}$ and $\frac{20}{38}$

14) $\frac{10}{14}$ and $\frac{40}{56}$

15) $\frac{11}{13}$ and $\frac{44}{39}$

16) $\frac{15}{16}$ and $\frac{30}{32}$

17) $\frac{17}{19}$ and $\frac{34}{48}$

18) $\frac{5}{18}$ and $\frac{15}{54}$

19) $\frac{3}{14}$ and $\frac{18}{42}$

20) $\frac{7}{11}$ and $\frac{14}{32}$

21) $\frac{8}{11}$ and $\frac{32}{44}$

22) $\frac{8}{14}$ and $\frac{24}{54}$

✍ *Solve.*

23) The ratio of boys to girls in a class is $3:4$. If there are 27 boys in the class, how many girls are in that class? _____

24) The ratio of red marbles to blue marbles in a bag is $5:6$. If there are 66 marbles in the bag, how many of the marbles are red? _____

25) You can buy 6 cans of green beans at a supermarket for $3.60. How much does it cost to buy 48 cans of green beans? _____

bit.ly/37GHQxp

Find more at

Similarity and Ratios

✍ *Each pair of figures is similar. Find the missing side.*

1)

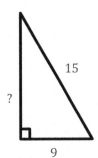

2)

3)

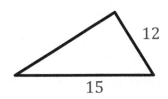

4)

✍ *Solve.*

5) Two rectangles are similar. The first is 6 feet wide and 20 feet long. The second is 15 feet wide. What is the length of the second rectangle? _____

6) Two rectangles are similar. One is 2.5 meters by 9 meters. The longer side of the second rectangle is 22.5 meters. What is the other side of the second rectangle?

_____

7) A building casts a shadow 24 ft long. At the same time a girl 5 ft tall casts a shadow 2 ft long. How tall is the building? _____

8) The scale of a map of Texas is 2 inches: 45 miles. If you measure the distance from Dallas to Martin County as 14.4 inches, approximately how far is Martin County from Dallas?

_____

Simple Interest

✎ *Determine the simple interest for these loans.*

1) $450 at 7% for 2 years. $ _____
2) $5,200 at 4% for 3 years. $ _____
3) $1,300 at 5% for 6 years. $ _____
4) $5,400 at 3.5% for 6 months. $ _____
5) $600 at 4% for 9 months. $ _____

6) $24,000 at 5.5% for 5 years. $ _____
7) $15,600 at 3% for 2 years. $ _____
8) $1,200 at 5.5% for 4 years. $ _____
9) $1,600 at 4.5% for 9 months. $ _____
10) $12,000 at 2.2% for 5 years. $ _____

✎ *Solve each simple interest word problem.*

11)　A new car, valued at $28,000, depreciates at 9% per year. What is the value of the car one year after purchase? $_____

12)　Sara puts $4,000 into an investment yielding 5% annual simple interest; she left the money in for five years. How much interest does Sara get at the end of those five years? $_____

13)　A bank is offering 3.5% simple interest on a savings account. If you deposit $7,500, how much interest will you earn in two years? $_____

14)　$400 interest is earned on a principal of $2,000 at a simple interest rate of 5% interest per year. For how many years was the principal invested? _____

15)　In how many years will $1,200 yield an interest of $180 at 3% simple interest? _____

16)　Jim invested $4,000 in a bond at a yearly rate of 4.5%. He earned $540 in interest. How long was the money invested? _____

Answers – Chapter 4

Simplifying Ratios

1) 3 : 2
2) 1 : 10
3) 1 : 12
4) 1 : 2
5) 3 : 50
6) 1 : 6
7) 3 : 7
8) 1 : 2
9) 1 : 5
10) 7 : 9
11) 5 : 3
12) 7 : 3
13) 10 : 1
14) 7 : 9
15) 2 : 5
16) 5 : 7
17) 7 : 9
18) 26 : 41

19) 1 : 3
20) 8 : 1
21) 1 : 2
22) 2 : 9
23) 17 : 20
24) 1 : 10
25) $\frac{1}{2}$
26) $\frac{3}{10}$
27) $\frac{1}{7}$
28) $\frac{2}{11}$
29) $\frac{1}{3}$
30) $\frac{3}{14}$
31) $\frac{1}{4}$
32) $\frac{3}{20}$

33) $\frac{5}{12}$
34) $\frac{9}{41}$
35) $\frac{11}{13}$
36) $\frac{2}{9}$
37) $\frac{1}{8}$
38) $\frac{2}{11}$
39) $\frac{1}{15}$
40) $\frac{1}{3}$
41) $\frac{4}{7}$
42) $\frac{3}{20}$
43) $\frac{22}{41}$
44) $\frac{1}{4}$
45) $\frac{1}{5}$

Proportional Ratios

1) 21
2) 40
3) 10
4) 18
5) 27
6) 42
7) 100
8) 9
9) 64
10) 63
11) 48
12) 16

13) Yes
14) Yes
15) Yes
16) No
17) No
18) No
19) Yes
20) Yes
21) No
22) No
23) Yes
24) Yes

25) 35
26) 42
27) 45
28) 16
29) 27
30) 52
31) 72
32) 77
33) 44
34) 55
35) 77
36) 45

Create Proportion

1) No
2) Yes
3) Yes
4) No
5) Yes
6) No
7) Yes
8) No
9) Yes
10) Yes
11) Yes
12) No
13) No
14) Yes
15) No
16) Yes
17) No
18) Yes
19) No
20) No
21) Yes
22) No
23) 36 *girls*
24) 30 *red marbles*
25) $28.80

Similarity and ratios

1) 12
2) 2
3) 5
4) 15
5) 50 feet
6) 6.25 meters
7) 60 feet
8) 324 miles

Simple Interest

1) $63.00
2) $624.00
3) $390.00
4) $94.50
5) $18.00
6) $6,600.00
7) $936.00
8) $264.00
9) $54.00
10) $1,320.00
11) $25,480.00
12) $1,000.00
13) $525.00
14) 4 years
15) 5 years
16) 3 years

Chapter 5: Percentage

Math Topics that you'll learn in this Chapter:

✓ Percent Problems

✓ Percent of Increase and Decrease

✓ Discount, Tax and Tip

35

Percent Problems

✍ *Solve each problem.*

1) 20 is what percent of 50? ____%

2) 18 is what percent of 90? ____%

3) 12 is what percent of 15? ____%

4) 16 is what percent of 200? ____%

5) 24 is what percent of 800? ____%

6) 48 is what percent of 400? ____%

7) 90 is what percent of 750? ____%

8) 24 is what percent of 300? ____%

9) 60 is what percent of 400? ____%

10) 42 is what percent of 350? ___%

11) 11 is what percent of 44? ___%

12) 8 is what percent of 64? ____%

13) 210 is what percent of 875? ___%

14) 80 is what percent of 64? ____%

15) 15 is what percent of 12? ___%

16) 56 is what percent of 40? ___%

17) 36 is what percent of 240? ___%

18) 32 is what percent of 20? ___%

✍ *Solve each percent word problem.*

19) There are **48** employees in a company. On a certain day, **36** were present. What percent showed up for work? _____%

20) A metal bar weighs **24** ounces. 15% of the bar is gold. How many ounces of gold are in the bar? _____

21) A crew is made up of **12** women; the rest are men. If **20%** of the crew are women, how many people are in the crew? _____

22) There are **48** students in a class and **6** of them are girls. What percent are boys? _____%

23) The Royals softball team played **75** games and won **60** of them. What percent of the games did they lose? _____%

Percent of Increase and Decrease

Find each percent of change.

1) From 200 to 500.   ___ %

2) From 50 ft to 75 ft.   ___ %

3) From $250 to $350.   ___ %

4) From 60 cm to 90 cm. ___ %

5) From 30 to 90.   ___ %

6) From 30 to 6.   ___ %

7) From 80 to 120.   ___ %

8) From 800 to 200.   ___ %

9) From 25 to 15.   ___ %

10) From 32 to 8.   ___ %

Solve each percent of change word problem.

11) Bob got a raise, and his hourly wage increased from $12 to $15. What is the percent increase? _____ %

12) The price of a pair of shoes increases from $20 to $32. What is the percent increase? ___ %

13) At a coffeeshop, the price of a cup of coffee increased from $1.20 to $1.44. What is the percent increase in the cost of the coffee? _____ %

14) 6 cm are cut from a 24 cm board. What is the percent decrease in length? _____ %

15) In a class, the number of students has been increased from 18 to 27. What is the percent increase? _____ %

16) The price of gasoline rose from $2.40 to $2.76 in one month. By what percent did the gas price rise? _____ %

17) A shirt was originally priced at $48. It went on sale for $38.40. What was the percent that the shirt was discounted? _____ %

bit.ly/3pgPQes

Find more at

Discount, Tax and Tip

✎ *Find the selling price of each item.*

1) Original price of a computer: $500

   Tax: 6%   Selling price: $_____

2) Original price of a laptop: $350

   Tax: 8%   Selling price: $_____

3) Original price of a sofa: $800

   Tax: 7%   Selling price: $_____

4) Original price of a car: $18,500

   Tax: 8.5%   Selling price: $_____

5) Original price of a Table: $250

   Tax: 5%   Selling price: $_____

6) Original price of a house: $250,000

   Tax: 6.5%   Selling price: $_____

7) Original price of a tablet: $400

   Discount: 20%   Selling price: $_____

8) Original price of a chair: $150

   Discount: 15%   Selling price: $_____

9) Original price of a book: $50

   Discount: 25%   Selling price: $_____

10) Original price of a cellphone: $500

   Discount: 10%   Selling price: $_____

11) Food bill: $24

   Tip: 20%   Price: $_____

12) Food bill: $60

   Tipp: 15%   Price: $_____

13) Food bill: $32

   Tip: 20%   Price: $_____

14) Food bill: $18

   Tipp: 25%   Price: $_____

✎ *Solve each word problem.*

15) Nicolas hired a moving company. The company charged $400 for its services, and Nicolas gives the movers a 15% tip. How much does Nicolas tip the movers? $_____

16) Mason has lunch at a restaurant and the cost of his meal is $30. Mason wants to leave a 20% tip. What is Mason's total bill including tip? $_____

17) The sales tax in Texas is 8.25% and an item costs $400. How much is the tax? $_____

18) The price of a table at Best Buy is $220. If the sales tax is 6%, what is the final price of the table including tax? $_____

Answers – Chapter 5

Percent Problems

1) 40%	9) 15%	17) 15%
2) 20%	10) 12%	18) 160%
3) 80%	11) 25%	19) 75%
4) 8%	12) 12.5%	20) 3.6 ounces
5) 3%	13) 24%	21) 60
6) 12%	14) 125%	22) 87.5%
7) 12%	15) 125%	23) 20%
8) 8%	16) 140%	

Percent of Increase and Decrease

1) 150%	7) 50%	13) 20%
2) 50%	8) 75%	14) 25%
3) 40%	9) 40%	15) 50%
4) 50%	10) 75%	16) 15%
5) 200%	11) 25%	17) 20%
6) 80%	12) 60%	

Discount, Tax and Tip

1) $530.00	7) $320.00	13) $38.40
2) $378.00	8) $127.50	14) $22.50
3) $856.00	9) $37.50	15) $60.00
4) $20,072.50	10) $450.00	16) $36.00
5) $262.50	11) $28.80	17) $33.00
6) $266,250	12) $69.00	18) $233.20

Effortless Math Education

Chapter 6: Expressions and Variables

Math Topics that you'll learn in this Chapter:

- ✓ Simplifying Variable Expressions
- ✓ Simplifying Polynomial Expressions
- ✓ Evaluating One Variable
- ✓ Evaluating Two Variables
- ✓ The Distributive Property

41

Simplifying Variable Expressions

✎ *Simplify each expression.*

1) $3(x + 9) =$

2) $(-6)(8x - 4) =$

3) $7x + 3 - 3x =$

4) $-2 - x^2 - 6x^2 =$

5) $3 + 10x^2 + 2 =$

6) $8x^2 + 6x + 7x^2 =$

7) $5x^2 - 12x^2 + 8x =$

8) $2x^2 - 2x - x =$

9) $4x + 6(2 - 5x) =$

10) $10x + 8(10x - 6) =$

11) $9(-2x - 6) - 5 =$

12) $2x^2 + (-8x) =$

13) $x - 3 + 5 - 3x =$

14) $2 - 3x + 12 - 2x =$

15) $32x - 4 + 23 + 2x =$

16) $(-6)(8x - 4) + 10x =$

17) $14x - 5(5 - 8x) =$

18) $23x + 4(9x + 3) + 12 =$

19) $3(-7x + 5) + 20x =$

20) $12x - 3x(x + 9) =$

21) $7x + 5x(3 - 3x) =$

22) $5x(-8x + 12) + 14x =$

23) $40x + 12 + 2x^2 =$

24) $5x(x - 3) - 10 =$

25) $8x - 7 + 8x + 2x^2 =$

26) $2x^2 - 5x - 7x =$

27) $7x - 3x^2 - 5x^2 - 3 =$

28) $4 + x^2 - 6x^2 - 12x =$

29) $12x + 8x^2 + 2x + 20 =$

30) $2x^2 + 6x + 3x^2 =$

31) $23 + 15x^2 + 8x - 4x^2 =$

32) $8x - 12x - x^2 + 13 =$

Simplifying Polynomial Expressions

✎ *Simplify each polynomial.*

1) $(2x^3 + 5x^2) - (12x + 2x^2) =$ _____

2) $(2x^5 + 2x^3) - (7x^3 + 6x^2) =$ _____

3) $(12x^4 + 4x^2) - (2x^2 - 6x^4) =$ _____

4) $14x - 3x^2 - 2(6x^2 + 6x^3) =$ _____

5) $(5x^3 - 3) + 5(2x^2 - 3x^3) =$ _____

6) $(4x^3 - 2x) - 2(4x^3 - 2x^4) =$ _____

7) $2(4x - 3x^3) - 3(3x^3 + 4x^2) =$ _____

8) $(2x^2 - 2x) - (2x^3 + 5x^2) =$ _____

9) $2x^3 - (4x^4 + 2x) + x^2 =$ _____

10) $x^4 - 2(x^2 + x) + 3x =$ _____

11) $(2x^2 - x^4) - (4x^4 - x^2) =$ _____

12) $4x^2 - 5x^3 + 15x^4 - 12x^3 =$ _____

13) $2x^2 - 5x^4 + 14x^4 - 11x^3 =$ _____

14) $2x^2 + 5x^3 - 7x^2 + 12x =$ _____

15) $2x^4 - 5x^5 + 8x^4 - 8x^2 =$ _____

16) $5x^3 + 15x - x^2 - 2x^3 =$ _____

Evaluating One Variable

✏️ *Evaluate each expression using the value given.*

1) $5 + x$, $x = 2$

2) $x - 2$, $x = 4$

3) $8x + 1$, $x = 9$

4) $x - 12$, $x = -1$

5) $9 - x$, $x = 3$

6) $x + 2$, $x = 5$

7) $3x + 7$, $x = 6$

8) $x + (-5)$, $x = -2$

9) $3x + 6$, $x = 4$

10) $4x + 6$, $x = -1$

11) $10 + 2x - 6$, $x = 3$

12) $10 - 3x$, $x = 8$

13) $2x - 5$, $x = 4$

14) $5x + 6$, $x = -3$

15) $12x + 6$, $x = 2$

16) $10 - 3x$, $x = -2$

17) $5(6x + 2)$, $x = 8$

18) $2(-7x - 2)$, $x = 3$

19) $9x - 3x + 12$, $x = 6$

20) $(6x + 3) \div 5$, $x = 2$

21) $(x + 16) \div 3$, $x = 8$

22) $4x - 12 + 8x$, $x = -6$

23) $(16 - 12x)(-2)$, $x = -3$

24) $12x^2 + 5x - 3$, $x = 2$

25) $x^2 - 11x$, $x = -4$

26) $2x(6 - 4x)$, $x = 5$

27) $14x + 7 - 3x^2$, $x = -3$

28) $(-5)(10x - 20 + 2x)$, $x = 2$

29) $(-3) + \frac{x}{4} + 2x$, $x = 16$

30) $(-2) + \frac{x}{7}$, $x = 21$

31) $\left(-\frac{14}{x}\right) - 9 + 4x$, $x = 2$

32) $\left(-\frac{6}{x}\right) - 9 + 2x$, $x = 3$

Evaluating Two Variables

✎ *Evaluate each expression using the values given.*

1) $2x + 4y,$

   $x = 3, y = 2$

2) $8x + 5y,$

   $x = 1, y = 5$

3) $-2a + 4b,$

   $a = 6, b = 3$

4) $4x + 7 - 2y,$

   $x = 7, y = 6$

5) $5z + 12 - 4k,$

   $z = 5 , k = 2$

6) $2(-x - 2y),$

   $x = 6, y = 9$

7) $18a + 2b,$

   $a = 2, b = 8$

8) $4x \div 3y,$

   $x = 3, y = 2$

9) $2x + 15 + 4y,$

   $x = -2, y = 4$

10) $4a - (15 - b),$

   $a = 4, b = 6$

11) $5z + 19 + 8k,$

   $z = -5, k = 4$

12) $xy + 12 + 5x,$

   $x = 7, y = 2$

13) $2x + 4y - 3 + 2,$

   $x = 5, y = 3$

14) $\left(-\frac{12}{x}\right) + 1 + 5y,$

   $x = 6, y = 8$

15) $(-4)(-2a - 2b),$

   $a = 5, b = 3$

16) $10 + 3x + 7 - 2y,$

   $x = 7, y = 6$

17) $9x + 2 - 4y + 5,$

   $x = 7, y = 5$

18) $6 + 3(-2x - 3y),$

   $x = 9, y = 7$

19) $2x + 14 + 4y,$

   $x = 6, y = 8$

20) $4a - (5a - b) + 5,$

   $a = 4, b = 6$

The Distributive Property

 Use the distributive property to simply each expression.

1) $2(2 + 3x) =$

2) $3(5 + 5x) =$

3) $4(3x - 8) =$

4) $(6x - 2)(-2) =$

5) $(-3)(x + 2) =$

6) $(2 + 2x)5 =$

7) $(-4)(4 - 2x) =$

8) $-(-2 - 5x) =$

9) $(-6x + 2)(-1) =$

10) $(-5)(x - 2) =$

11) $-(7 - 3x) =$

12) $8(8 + 2x) =$

13) $2(12 + 2x) =$

14) $(-6x + 8)4 =$

15) $(3 - 6x)(-7) =$

16) $(-12)(2x + 1) =$

17) $(8 - 2x)9 =$

18) $5(7 + 9x) =$

19) $11(5x + 2) =$

20) $(-4x + 6)6 =$

21) $(3 - 6x)(-8) =$

22) $(-12)(2x - 3) =$

23) $(10 - 2x)9 =$

24) $(-5)(11x - 2) =$

25) $(1 - 9x)(-10) =$

26) $(-6)(x + 8) =$

27) $(-4 + 3x)(-8) =$

28) $(-5)(1 - 11x) =$

29) $11(3x - 12) =$

30) $(-12x + 14)(-5) =$

31) $(-5)(4x - 1) + 4(x + 2) =$

32) $(-3)(x + 4) - (2 + 3x) =$

Answers – Chapter 6

Simplifying Variable Expressions

1) $3x + 27$
2) $-48x + 24$
3) $4x + 3$
4) $-7x^2 - 2$
5) $10x^2 + 5$
6) $15x^2 + 6x$
7) $-7x^2 + 8x$
8) $2x^2 - 3x$
9) $-26x + 12$
10) $90x - 48$

11) $-18x - 59$
12) $2x^2 - 8x$
13) $-2x + 2$
14) $-5x + 14$
15) $34x + 19$
16) $-38x + 24$
17) $54x - 25$
18) $59x + 24$
19) $-x + 15$
20) $-3x^2 - 15x$
21) $-15x^2 + 22x$

22) $-40x^2 + 74x$
23) $2x^2 + 40x + 12$
24) $5x^2 - 15x - 10$
25) $2x^2 + 16x - 7$
26) $2x^2 - 12x$
27) $-8x^2 + 7x - 3$
28) $-5x^2 - 12x + 4$
29) $8x^2 + 14x + 20$
30) $5x^2 + 6x$
31) $11x^2 + 8x + 23$
32) $-x^2 - 4x + 13$

Simplifying Polynomial Expressions

1) $2x^3 + 3x^2 - 12x$
2) $2x^5 - 5x^3 - 6x^2$
3) $18x^4 + 2x^2$
4) $-12x^3 - 15x^2 + 14x$
5) $-10x^3 + 10x^2 - 3$
6) $4x^4 - 4x^3 - 2x$
7) $-15x^3 - 12x^2 + 8x$
8) $-2x^3 - 3x^2 - 2x$

9) $-4x^4 + 2x^3 + x^2 - 2x$
10) $x^4 - 2x^2 + x$
11) $-5x^4 + 3x^2$
12) $15x^4 - 17x^3 + 4x^2$
13) $9x^4 - 11x^3 + 2x^2$
14) $5x^3 - 5x^2 + 12x$
15) $-5x^5 + 10x^4 - 8x^2$
16) $3x^3 - x^2 + 15x$

Evaluating One Variables

1) 7
2) 2
3) 73
4) -13
5) 6
6) 7
7) 25
8) -7
9) 18
10) 2
11) 10

12) -14
13) 3
14) -9
15) 30
16) 16
17) 250
18) -46
19) 48
20) 3
21) 8
22) -84

23) -104
24) 55
25) 60
26) -140
27) -62
28) -20
29) 33
30) 1
31) -8
32) -5

Evaluating Two Variables

1) 14
2) 33

3) 0
4) 23

5) 29
6) -48

Effortless Math Education

7) 52
8) 2
9) 27
10) 7
11) 26
12) 61

13) 21
14) 39
15) 64
16) 26
17) 50

18) −111
19) 58
20) 7

The Distributive Property

1) $6x + 4$
2) $15x + 15$
3) $12x - 32$
4) $-12x + 4$
5) $-3x - 6$
6) $10x + 10$
7) $8x - 16$
8) $5x + 2$
9) $6x - 2$
10) $-5x + 10$
11) $3x - 7$

12) $16x + 64$
13) $4x + 24$
14) $-24x + 32$
15) $42x - 21$
16) $-24x - 12$
17) $-18x + 72$
18) $45x + 35$
19) $55x + 22$
20) $-24x + 36$
21) $48x - 24$
22) $-24x + 36$

23) $-18x + 90$
24) $-55x + 10$
25) $90x - 10$
26) $-6x - 48$
27) $-24x + 32$
28) $55x - 5$
29) $33x - 132$
30) $60x - 70$
31) $-16x + 13$
32) $-6x - 14$

Chapter 7: Equations and Inequalities

Math Topics that you'll learn in this Chapter:

- ✓ One–Step Equations
- ✓ Multi–Step Equations
- ✓ System of Equations
- ✓ Graphing Single–Variable Inequalities
- ✓ One–Step Inequalities
- ✓ Multi–Step Inequalities

49

One–Step Equations

✑ *Solve each equation.*

1) $2x = 20, x =$ ____

2) $4x = 16, x =$ ____

3) $8x = 24, x =$ ____

4) $6x = 30, x =$ ____

5) $x + 5 = 8, x =$ ____

6) $x - 1 = 5, x =$ ____

7) $x - 8 = 3, x =$ ____

8) $x + 6 = 12, x =$ ____

9) $x - 2 = 17, x =$ ____

10) $8 = 12 + x, x =$ ____

11) $x - 5 = 4, x =$ ____

12) $2 - x = -12, x =$ ____

13) $16 = -4 + x, x =$ ____

14) $x - 4 = -25, x =$ ____

15) $x + 12 = -9, x =$ ____

16) $14 = 18 - x, x =$ ____

17) $2 + x = -14, x =$ ____

18) $x - 5 = 15, x =$ ____

19) $25 = x - 5, x =$ ____

20) $x - 3 = -12, x =$ ____

21) $x - 12 = 12, x =$ ____

22) $x - 12 = -25, x =$ ____

23) $x - 13 = 32, x =$ ____

24) $-55 = x - 18, x =$ ____

25) $x - 12 = 18, x =$ ____

26) $20 = 5x, x =$ ____

27) $x - 30 = 20, x =$ ____

28) $x - 12 = 32, x =$ ____

29) $36 - x = 3, x =$ ____

30) $x - 14 = 14, x =$ ____

31) $19 - x = -15, x =$ ____

32) $x - 19 = -35, x =$ ____

Multi–Step Equations

✍ *Solve each equation.*

1) $2x + 3 = 5$

2) $-x + 8 = 5$

3) $3x - 4 = 5$

4) $-(2 - x) = 5$

5) $2x - 18 = 12$

6) $4x - 2 = 6$

7) $2x - 14 = 4$

8) $5x + 10 = 25$

9) $8x + 9 = 25$

10) $-3(2 + x) = 3$

11) $-2(4 + x) = 4$

12) $20 = -(x - 8)$

13) $2(2 - 2x) = 20$

14) $-12 = -(2x + 8)$

15) $5(2 + x) = 5$

16) $2(x - 14) = 4$

17) $-28 = 2x + 12x$

18) $3x + 15 = -x - 5$

19) $2(3 + 2x) = -18$

20) $12 - 2x = -8 - x$

21) $10 - 3x = 14 + x$

22) $10 + 10x = -2 + 4x$

23) $24 = (-4x) - 8 + 8$

24) $12 = 2x - 12 + 6x$

25) $-12 = -4x - 6 + 2x$

26) $4x - 12 = -18 + 5x$

27) $5x - 10 = 2x + 5$

28) $-7 - 3x = 2(3 - 2x)$

29) $x - 2 = -3(6 - 3x)$

30) $10x - 56 = 12x - 114$

31) $4x - 8 = -4(11 + 2x)$

32) $-5x - 14 = 6x + 52$

Systems of Equations

✎ *Solve each system of equations.*

1) $-2x + 2y = 4$ $x =$ ___
   $-2x + y = 3$ $y =$ ___

2) $-10x + 2y = -6$ $x =$ ___
   $6x - 16y = 48$ $y =$ ___

3) $y = -8$ $x =$ ___
   $16x - 12y = 32$

4) $2y = -6x + 10$ $x =$ ___
   $10x - 8y = -6$ $y =$ ___

5) $10x - 9y = -13$ $x =$ ___
   $-5x + 3y = 11$ $y =$ ___

6) $-3x - 4y = 5$ $x =$ ___
   $x - 2y = 5$ $y =$ ___

7) $5x - 14y = -23$ $x =$ ___
   $-6x + 7y = 8$ $y =$ ___

8) $10x - 14y = -4$ $x =$ ___
   $-10x - 20y = -30$ $y =$ ___

9) $-4x + 12y = 12$ $x =$ ___
   $-14x + 16y = -10$ $y =$ ___

10) $x + 20y = 56$ $x =$ ___
    $x + 15y = 41$ $y =$ ___

11) $6x - 7y = -8$ $x =$ ___
    $-x - 4y = -9$ $y =$ ___

12) $-3x + 2y = -18$ $x =$ ___
    $8x - 2y = 28$ $y =$ ___

13) $-5x + y = -3$ $x =$ ___
    $3x - 8y = 24$ $y =$ ___

14) $3x - 2y = 2$ $x =$ ___
    $5x - 5y = 10$ $y =$ ___

15) $8x + 14y = 4$ $x =$ ___
    $-6x - 7y = -10$ $y =$ ___

16) $10x + 7y = 1$ $x =$ ___
    $-5x - 7y = 24$ $y =$ ___

Graphing Single–Variable Inequalities

✏️ *Draw a graph for each inequality.*

1) $x > 2$

2) $x < 5$

3) $x > -1$

4) $x < 3$
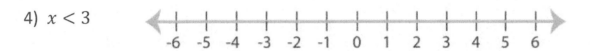

5) $x < -5$

6) $x > -2$

7) $x < 0$

8) $x > 4$

One–Step Inequalities

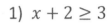 *Solve each inequality and graph it.*

1) $x + 2 \geq 3$

2) $x - 1 \leq 2$

3) $2x \geq 12$
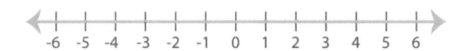

4) $4 + x \leq 5$

5) $x + 3 \leq -3$

6) $4x \geq 16$

7) $9x \leq 18$
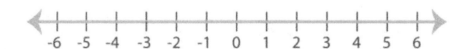

8) $x + 2 \geq 7$

Multi-Step Inequalities

✎ *Solve each inequality.*

1) $x - 2 \leq 6$

2) $3 - x \leq 3$

3) $2x - 4 \leq 8$

4) $3x - 5 \geq 16$

5) $x - 5 \geq 10$

6) $2x - 8 \leq 6$

7) $8x - 2 \leq 14$

8) $-5 + 3x \leq 10$

9) $2(x - 3) \leq 6$

10) $7x - 5 \leq 9$

11) $4x - 21 < 19$

12) $2x - 3 < 21$

13) $17 - 3x \geq -13$

14) $9 + 4x < 21$

15) $3 + 2x \geq 19$

16) $6 + 2x < 32$

17) $4x - 1 < 7$

18) $3(3 - 2x) \geq -15$

19) $-(3 + 4x) < 13$

20) $20 - 8x \geq -28$

21) $-3(x - 7) > 21$

22) $\dfrac{2x+6}{4} \leq 10$

23) $\dfrac{4x+8}{2} \leq 12$

24) $\dfrac{3x-8}{7} > 1$

25) $4 + \dfrac{x}{3} < 7$

26) $\dfrac{9x}{7} - 7 < 2$

27) $\dfrac{4x+12}{4} > 1$

28) $15 + \dfrac{x}{5} < 12$

Answers – Chapter 7

One–Step Equations

1) 10	12) 14	23) 45
2) 4	13) 20	24) −37
3) 3	14) −21	25) 30
4) 5	15) −21	26) 4
5) 3	16) 4	27) 50
6) 6	17) −16	28) 44
7) 11	18) 20	29) 33
8) 6	19) 30	30) 28
9) 19	20) −9	31) 34
10) −4	21) 24	32) −16
11) 9	22) −13	

Multi–Step Equations

1) 1	12) −12	23) −6
2) 3	13) −4	24) 3
3) 3	14) 2	25) 3
4) 7	15) −1	26) 6
5) 15	16) 16	27) 5
6) 2	17) −2	28) 13
7) 9	18) −5	29) 2
8) 3	19) −6	30) 29
9) 2	20) 20	31) −3
10) −3	21) −1	32) −6
11) −6	22) −2	

Systems of Equations

1) $x = -1, y = 1$	7) $x = 1, y = 2$	13) $x = 0, y = -3$
2) $x = 0, y = -3$	8) $x = 1, y = 1$	14) $x = -2, y = -4$
3) $x = -4$	9) $x = 3, y = 2$	15) $x = 4, y = -2$
4) $x = 1, y = 2$	10) $x = -4, y = 3$	16) $x = 5, y = -7$
5) $x = -4, y = -3$	11) $x = 1, y = 2$	
6) $x = 1, y = -2$	12) $x = 2, y = -6$	

Graphing Single–Variable Inequalities

1)

2)
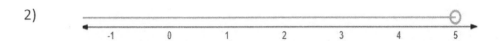

3)

4)
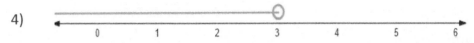

5)

6)
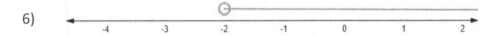

7)

8)
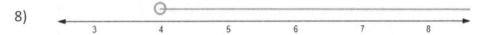

One–Step Inequalities

1)
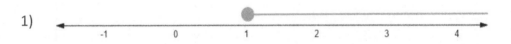

2)

3)

4)

Effortless Math Education

5)

6)

7)

8)

Multi-Step Inequalities

1) $x \le 8$
2) $x \ge 0$
3) $x \le 6$
4) $x \ge 7$
5) $x \ge 15$
6) $x \le 7$
7) $x \le 2$
8) $x \le 5$
9) $x \le 6$
10) $x \le 2$

11) $x < 10$
12) $x < 12$
13) $x \le 10$
14) $x < 3$
15) $x \ge 8$
16) $x < 13$
17) $x < 2$
18) $x \le 4$
19) $x > -4$
20) $x \le 6$

21) $x < 0$
22) $x \le 17$
23) $x \le 4$
24) $x > 5$
25) $x < 9$
26) $x < 7$
27) $x > -2$
28) $x < -15$

Chapter 8: Lines and Slope

Math Topics that you'll learn in this Chapter:

- ✓ Finding Slope
- ✓ Graphing Lines Using Slope–Intercept Form
- ✓ Writing Linear Equations
- ✓ Graphing Linear Inequalities
- ✓ Finding Midpoint
- ✓ Finding Distance of Two Points

Finding Slope

✎ **Find the slope of each line.**

1) $y = x - 1$

2) $y = -2x + 5$

3) $y = 2x - 1$

4) $y = -x - 8$

5) $y = 6 + 5x$

6) $y = 2 - 3x$

7) $y = 4x + 12$

8) $y = -6x + 2$

9) $y = -x + 8$

10) $y = 7x - 5$

11) $y = \frac{1}{2}x + 3$

12) $y = -\frac{2}{3}x + 1$

13) $-x + 2y = 5$

14) $2x + 2y = 6$

15) $8y - 2x = 10$

16) $5y - x = 2$

✎ **Find the slope of the line through each pair of points.**

17) $(1, 1), (2, 3)$

18) $(-1, 2), (0, 3)$

19) $(3, -1), (2, 3)$

20) $(-2, -1), (0, 5)$

21) $(5, 1), (2, 4)$

22) $(-3, 1), (-2, 4)$

23) $(6, 2), (7, 4)$

24) $(6, -5), (3, 4)$

25) $(12, -9), (11, -8)$

26) $(7, 4), (5, -2)$

27) $(1, 1), (3, 5)$

28) $(7, -12), (5, 10)$

Graphing Lines Using Slope–Intercept Form

✎ *Sketch the graph of each line.*

1) $y = 3x - 2$ 2) $y = -x + 1$ 3) $x + y = 4$

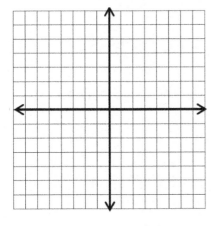 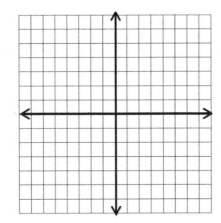 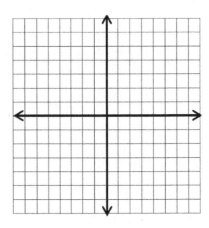

4) $x - y = -5$ 5) $2x - y = -4$ 6) $3x - 2y = -6$

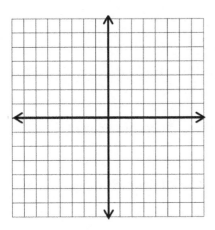 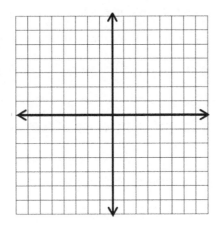 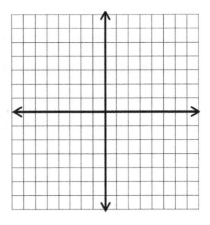

bit.ly/3hfdnJL

Find more at

Writing Linear Equations

✍ **Write the equation of the line through the given points.**

1) through: $(1, -2), (2, 3)$

2) through: $(-2, 1), (1, 4)$

3) through: $(-2, 1), (0, 5)$

4) through: $(5, 4), (2, 1)$

5) through: $(-4, 9), (3, 2)$

6) through: $(8, 3), (7, 2)$

7) through: $(7, -2), (5, 2)$

8) through: $(-3, 9), (5, -7)$

9) through: $(6, 8), (4, 14)$

10) through: $(5, 9), (7, -3)$

11) through: $(-2, 8), (-6, -4)$

12) through: $(3, 3), (1, -5)$

13) through: $(8, -5), (-5, 8)$

14) through: $(2, -6), (-1, 3)$

15) through: $(5, 5), (2, -4)$

16) through: $(-1, 8), (2, -7)$

✍ **Solve each problem.**

17) What is the equation of a line with slope 2 and intercept 4? _____

18) What is the equation of a line with slope 4 and intercept 12? _____

19) What is the equation of a line with slope 4 and passes through point $(4, 2)$?

_____

20) What is the equation of a line with slope -2 and passes through point $(-2, 4)$?

_____

21) The slope of a line is -3 and it passes through point $(-1, 5)$. What is the equation of the line? _____

22) The slope of a line is 3 and it passes through point $(-1, 4)$. What is the equation of the line? _____

Graphing Linear Inequalities

✍ *Sketch the graph of each linear inequality.*

1) $y > 3x - 1$ 2) $y < -x + 4$ 3) $y \leq -5x + 8$

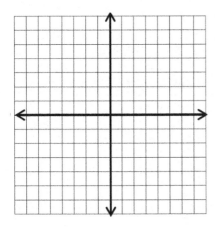 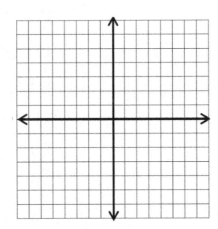 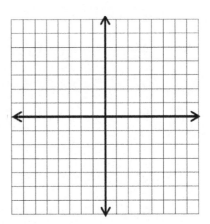

4) $2y \geq 8 + 6x$ 5) $y < 2x - 3$ 6) $4y \leq -6x + 2$

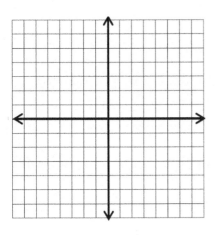 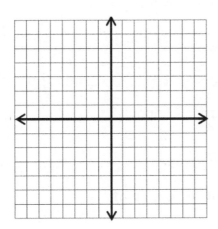 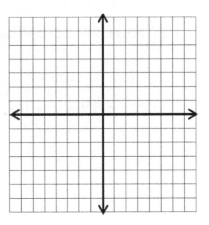

Finding Midpoint

✎ **Find the midpoint of the line segment with the given endpoints.**

1) $(-2, -2), (0, 2)$

2) $(5, 1), (-2, 4)$

3) $(4, -1), (0, 3)$

4) $(-3, 5), (-1, 3)$

5) $(3, -2), (7, -6)$

6) $(-4, -3), (2, -7)$

7) $(5, 0), (-5, 8)$

8) $(-6, 4), (-2, 0)$

9) $(-3, 4), (9, -6)$

10) $(2, 8), (6, -2)$

11) $(4, 7), (-6, 5)$

12) $(9, 3), (-1, -7)$

13) $(-4, 12), (-2, 6)$

14) $(14, 5), (8, -1)$

15) $(11, 7), (-3, 1)$

16) $(-7, -4), (-3, 8)$

17) $(13, 7), (5, 11)$

18) $(-5, -10), (9, -2)$

19) $(8, 15), (-2, 7)$

20) $(13, -2), (5, 10)$

21) $(2, -2), (3, -5)$

22) $(0, 2), (-2, -6)$

23) $(7, 4), (9, -1)$

24) $(4, -5), (0, 8)$

✎ **Solve each problem.**

25) One endpoint of a line segment is $(1, 2)$ and the midpoint of the line segment is $(-1, 4)$. What is the other endpoint? _____

26) One endpoint of a line segment is $(-3, 6)$ and the midpoint of the line segment is $(5, 2)$. What is the other endpoint? _____

27) One endpoint of a line segment is $(-2, -6)$ and the midpoint of the line segment is $(6, 8)$. What is the other endpoint? _____

Finding Distance of Two Points

✎ *Find the distance between each pair of points.*

1) $(2, 1), (-1, -3)$

2) $(-2, -1), (2, 2)$

3) $(-1, 0), (5, 8)$

4) $(-4, -1), (1, 11)$

5) $(3, -2), (-6, -14)$

6) $(-6, 0), (-2, 3)$

7) $(3, 2), (11, 17)$

8) $(-6, -10), (6, -1)$

9) $(5, 9), (-11, -3)$

10) $(9, -3), (3, -11)$

11) $(2, 0), (12, 24)$

12) $(8, 4), (3, -8)$

13) $(4, 2), (-5, -10)$

14) $(-5, 6), (3, 21)$

15) $(0, 8), (-4, 5)$

16) $(-8, -5), (4, 0)$

17) $(3, 5), (-5, -10)$

18) $(-2, 3), (22, 13)$

19) $(7, 2), (-8, -18)$

20) $(-5, 4), (7, 9)$

✎ *Solve each problem.*

21) Triangle ABC is a right triangle on the coordinate system and its vertices are $(-2, 5)$, $(-2, 1)$, and $(1, 1)$. What is the area of triangle ABC? _____

22) Three vertices of a triangle on a coordinate system are $(1, 1)$, $(1, 4)$, and $(5, 4)$. What is the perimeter of the triangle? _____

23) Four vertices of a rectangle on a coordinate system are $(2, 5)$, $(2, 2)$, $(6, 5)$, and $(6, 2)$. What is its perimeter? _____

bit.ly/2KV50Hy

Find more at

Answers – Chapter 8

Finding Slope

1) 1
2) −2
3) 2
4) −1
5) 5
6) −3
7) 4
8) −6
9) −1
10) 7

11) $\frac{1}{2}$
12) $-\frac{2}{3}$
13) $\frac{1}{2}$
14) −1
15) $\frac{1}{4}$
16) $\frac{1}{5}$
17) 2
18) 1

19) −4
20) 3
21) −1
22) 3
23) 2
24) −3
25) −1
26) 3
27) 2
28) −11

Graphing Lines Using Slope–Intercept Form

1) $y = 3x - 2$

2) $y = -x + 1$

3) $x + y = 4$

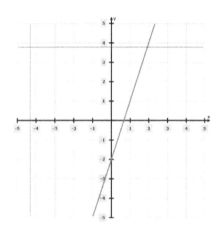
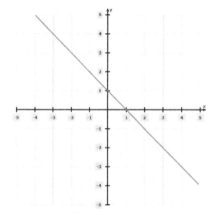
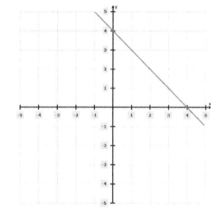

4) $x - y = -5$ 5) $2x - y = -4$ 6) $3x - 2y = -6$

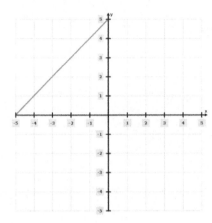   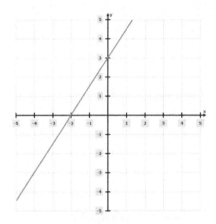

Writing Linear Equations

1) $y = 5x - 7$
2) $y = x + 3$
3) $y = 2x + 5$
4) $y = x - 1$
5) $y = -x + 5$
6) $y = x - 5$
7) $y = -2x + 12$
8) $y = -2x + 3$

9) $y = -3x + 26$
10) $y = -6x + 39$
11) $y = 3x + 14$
12) $y = 4x - 9$
13) $y = -x + 3$
14) $y = -3x$
15) $y = 3x - 10$
16) $y = -5x + 3$

17) $y = 2x + 4$
18) $y = 4x + 12$
19) $y = 4x - 14$
20) $y = -2x$
21) $y = -3x + 2$
22) $y = 3x + 7$

Graphing Linear Inequalities

1) $y > 3x - 1$ 2) $y < -x + 4$ 3) $y \leq -5x + 8$

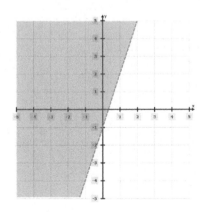   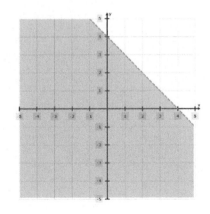   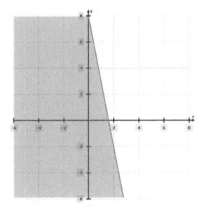

Effortless Math Education

4) $2y \geq 8 + 6x$ 5) $y < 2x - 3$ 6) $4y \leq -6x + 2$

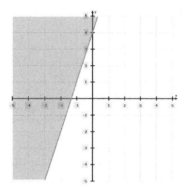

Finding Midpoint

1) $(-1, 0)$	10) $(4, 3)$	19) $(3, 11)$
2) $(1.5, 2.5)$	11) $(-1, 6)$	20) $(9, 4)$
3) $(2, 1)$	12) $(4, -2)$	21) $(2.5, -3.5)$
4) $(-2, 4)$	13) $(-3, 9)$	22) $(-1, -2)$
5) $(5, -4)$	14) $(11, 2)$	23) $(8, 1.5)$
6) $(-1, -5)$	15) $(4, 4)$	24) $(2, 1.5)$
7) $(0, 4)$	16) $(-5, 2)$	25) $(-3, 6)$
8) $(-4, 2)$	17) $(9, 9)$	26) $(13, -2)$
9) $(3, -1)$	18) $(2, -6)$	27) $(14, 22)$

Finding Distance of Two Points

1) 5	9) 20	17) 17
2) 5	10) 10	18) 26
3) 10	11) 26	19) 25
4) 13	12) 13	20) 13
5) 15	13) 15	21) 6 square units
6) 5	14) 17	22) 12 units
7) 17	15) 5	23) 14 units
8) 15	16) 13	

Chapter 9: Exponents and Variables

Math Topics that you'll learn in this Chapter:

- ✓ Multiplication Property of Exponents
- ✓ Division Property of Exponents
- ✓ Powers of Products and Quotients
- ✓ Zero and Negative Exponents
- ✓ Negative Exponents and Negative Bases
- ✓ Scientific Notation
- ✓ Radicals

Multiplication Property of Exponents

 Simplify and write the answer in exponential form.

1) $2 \times 2^2 =$

2) $5^3 \times 5 =$

3) $3^2 \times 3^2 =$

4) $4^2 \times 4^2 =$

5) $7^3 \times 7^2 \times 7 =$

6) $2 \times 2^2 \times 2^2 =$

7) $5^3 \times 5^2 \times 5 \times 5 =$

8) $2x \times x =$

9) $x^3 \times x^2 =$

10) $x^4 \times x^4 =$

11) $x^2 \times x^2 \times x^2 =$

12) $6x \times 6x =$

13) $2x^2 \times 2x^2 =$

14) $3x^2 \times x =$

15) $4x^4 \times 4x^4 \times 4x^4 =$

16) $2x^2 \times x^2 =$

17) $x^4 \times 3x =$

18) $x \times 2x^2 =$

19) $5x^4 \times 5x^4 =$

20) $2yx^2 \times 2x =$

21) $3x^4 \times y^2x^4 =$

22) $y^2x^3 \times y^5x^2 =$

23) $4yx^3 \times 2x^2y^3 =$

24) $6x^2 \times 6x^3y^4 =$

25) $3x^4y^5 \times 7x^2y^3 =$

26) $7x^2y^5 \times 9xy^3 =$

27) $7xy^4 \times 4x^3y^3 =$

28) $3x^5y^3 \times 8x^2y^3 =$

29) $3x \times y^5x^3 \times y^4 =$

30) $yx^2 \times 2y^2x^2 \times 2xy =$

31) $4yx^4 \times 5y^5x \times xy^3 =$

32) $7x^3 \times 10y^3x^5 \times 8yx^3 =$

Division Property of Exponents

✎ *Simplify.*

1) $\dfrac{2^2}{2^3} =$

2) $\dfrac{2^4}{2^2} =$

3) $\dfrac{5^5}{5} =$

4) $\dfrac{3}{3^5} =$

5) $\dfrac{x}{x^3} =$

6) $\dfrac{3 \times 3^3}{3^2 \times 3^4} =$

7) $\dfrac{5^8}{5^3} =$

8) $\dfrac{5 \times 5^6}{5^2 \times 5^7} =$

9) $\dfrac{3^4 \times 3^7}{3^2 \times 3^8} =$

10) $\dfrac{5x}{10x^3} =$

11) $\dfrac{3x^3}{2x^5} =$

12) $\dfrac{12x^3}{14x^6} =$

13) $\dfrac{12x^3}{9y^8} =$

14) $\dfrac{25xy^4}{5x^6y^2} =$

15) $\dfrac{2x^4}{7x} =$

16) $\dfrac{16x^2y^8}{4x^3} =$

17) $\dfrac{12x^4}{15x^7y^9} =$

18) $\dfrac{12yx^4}{10yx^8} =$

19) $\dfrac{16x^4y}{9x^8y^2} =$

20) $\dfrac{5x^8}{20x^8} =$

21) $\dfrac{2x^{-5}}{9x^{-2}} =$

Powers of Products and Quotients

✎ *Simplify.*

1) $(4^2)^2 =$

2) $(6^2)^3 =$

3) $(2 \times 2^3)^4 =$

4) $(4 \times 4^4)^2 =$

5) $(3^3 \times 3^2)^3 =$

6) $(5^4 \times 5^5)^2 =$

7) $(2 \times 2^4)^2 =$

8) $(2^6)^2 =$

9) $(11x^5)^2 =$

10) $(4x^2y^4)^4 =$

11) $(2x^4y^4)^3 =$

12) $(3x^2y^2)^2 =$

13) $(3x^4y^3)^4 =$

14) $(2x^6y^8)^2 =$

15) $(12x^3x)^3 =$

16) $(2x^9x^6)^3 =$

17) $(5x^{10}y^3)^3 =$

18) $(4x^3x^3)^2 =$

19) $(3x^3.5x)^2 =$

20) $(10x^{11}y^3)^2 =$

21) $(9x^7y^5)^2 =$

22) $(4x^4y^6)^5 =$

23) $(3x.4y^3)^2 =$

24) $\left(\frac{5x}{x^2}\right)^2 =$

25) $\left(\frac{x^4y^4}{x^2y^2}\right)^3 =$

26) $\left(\frac{25x}{5x^6}\right)^2 =$

27) $\left(\frac{x^8}{x^6y^2}\right)^2 =$

28) $\left(\frac{xy^2}{x^3y^3}\right)^{-2} =$

29) $\left(\frac{2xy^4}{x^3}\right)^2 =$

30) $\left(\frac{xy^4}{5xy^2}\right)^{-3} =$

Zero and Negative Exponents

✎ *Evaluate the following expressions.*

1) $1^{-1} =$

2) $2^{-2} =$

3) $0^{15} =$

4) $1^{-10} =$

5) $8^{-1} =$

6) $8^{-2} =$

7) $2^{-4} =$

8) $10^{-2} =$

9) $9^{-1} =$

10) $3^{-2} =$

11) $7^{-2} =$

12) $3^{-4} =$

13) $6^{-2} =$

14) $5^{-3} =$

15) $22^{-1=}$

16) $4^{-2} =$

17) $5^{-2} =$

18) $35^{-1} =$

19) $4^{-3} =$

20) $6^{-3} =$

21) $3^{-5} =$

22) $5^{-4} =$

23) $2^{-3} =$

24) $3^{-3} =$

25) $7^{-3} =$

26) $6^{-4} =$

27) $8^{-3} =$

28) $9^{-2} =$

29) $10^{-3} =$

30) $10^{-9} =$

31) $\left(\frac{1}{2}\right)^{-1} =$

32) $\left(\frac{1}{2}\right)^{-2} =$

33) $\left(\frac{1}{3}\right)^{-2} =$

34) $\left(\frac{2}{3}\right)^{-2} =$

35) $\left(\frac{1}{5}\right)^{-3} =$

36) $\left(\frac{3}{4}\right)^{-2} =$

37) $\left(\frac{2}{5}\right)^{-2} =$

38) $\left(\frac{1}{2}\right)^{-8} =$

39) $\left(\frac{2}{5}\right)^{-3} =$

40) $\left(\frac{3}{7}\right)^{-2} =$

41) $\left(\frac{5}{6}\right)^{-3} =$

42) $\left(\frac{4}{9}\right)^{-2} =$

Negative Exponents and Negative Bases

✍ *Simplify.*

1) $-6^{-1} =$

2) $-5^{-2} =$

3) $-2^{-4} =$

4) $-x^{-3} =$

5) $2x^{-1} =$

6) $-4x^{-3} =$

7) $-12x^{-5} =$

8) $-5x^{-2}y^{-3} =$

9) $20x^{-4}y^{-1} =$

10) $14a^{-6}b^{-7} =$

11) $-12x^2y^{-3} =$

12) $-\dfrac{25}{x^{-6}} =$

13) $-\dfrac{2x}{a^{-4}} =$

14) $\left(-\dfrac{1}{3}\right)^{-2} =$

15) $\left(-\dfrac{3}{4}\right)^{-2} =$

16) $-\dfrac{9}{a^{-7}b^{-2}} =$

17) $-\dfrac{5x}{x^{-3}} =$

18) $-\dfrac{a^{-3}}{b^{-2}} =$

19) $-\dfrac{5}{x^{-3}} =$

20) $\dfrac{7b}{-9c^{-4}} =$

21) $\dfrac{7ab}{a^{-3}b^{-1}} =$

22) $-\dfrac{5n^{-2}}{10p^{-3}} =$

23) $\dfrac{4ab^{-2}}{-3c^{-2}} =$

24) $\left(\dfrac{3a}{2c}\right)^{-2} =$

25) $\left(-\dfrac{5x}{3yz}\right)^{-3} =$

26) $\dfrac{4b^{-2}}{2c^3} =$

27) $\left(-\dfrac{x^3}{x^4}\right)^{-2} =$

28) $\left(-\dfrac{x^{-2}}{3x^2}\right)^{-3} =$

29) $\left(-\dfrac{x^{-4}}{x^2}\right)^{-2} =$

Scientific Notation

✎ *Write each number in scientific notation.*

1) $0.113 =$

2) $0.02 =$

3) $2.5 =$

4) $20 =$

5) $60 =$

6) $0.004 =$

7) $78 =$

8) $1,600 =$

9) $1,450 =$

10) $91,000 =$

11) $2,000,000 =$

12) $0.0000006 =$

13) $354,000 =$

14) $0.000325 =$

15) $0.00023 =$

16) $56,000,000 =$

17) $21,000 =$

18) $78,000,000 =$

19) $0.0000022 =$

20) $0.00012 =$

✎ *Write each number in standard notation.*

21) $3 \times 10^{-1} =$

22) $5 \times 10^{-2} =$

23) $1.2 \times 10^3 =$

24) $2 \times 10^{-4} =$

25) $1.5 \times 10^{-2} =$

26) $4 \times 10^3 =$

27) $9 \times 10^5 =$

28) $1.12 \times 10^4 =$

29) $3 \times 10^{-5} =$

30) $8.3 \times 10^{-5} =$

Radicals

✏️ *Simplify and write the answer.*

1) $\sqrt{0}$ = ____

2) $\sqrt{1}$ = ____

3) $\sqrt{4}$ = ____

4) $\sqrt{16}$ = ____

5) $\sqrt{9}$ = ____

6) $\sqrt{25}$ = ____

7) $\sqrt{49}$ = ____

8) $\sqrt{36}$ = ____

9) $\sqrt{64}$ = ____

10) $\sqrt{81}$ = ____

11) $\sqrt{121}$ = ____

12) $\sqrt{225}$ = ____

13) $\sqrt{144}$ = ____

14) $\sqrt{100}$ = ____

15) $\sqrt{256}$ = ____

16) $\sqrt{289}$ = ____

17) $\sqrt{324}$ = ____

18) $\sqrt{400}$ = ____

19) $\sqrt{900}$ = ____

20) $\sqrt{529}$ = ____

21) $\sqrt{90}$ = ____

22) $\sqrt{169}$ = ____

23) $\sqrt{196}$ = ____

24) $\sqrt{361}$ = ____

✏️ *Evaluate.*

25) $\sqrt{4} \times \sqrt{16}$ = _____

26) $\sqrt{25} \times \sqrt{64}$ = _____

27) $\sqrt{2} \times \sqrt{8}$ = _____

28) $\sqrt{6} \times \sqrt{6}$ = _____

29) $\sqrt{5} \times \sqrt{5}$ = _____

30) $\sqrt{8} \times \sqrt{8}$ = _____

31) $\sqrt{2} + \sqrt{2}$ = _____

32) $\sqrt{8} + \sqrt{8}$ = _____

33) $4\sqrt{5} - 2\sqrt{5}$ = _____

34) $3\sqrt{3} \times 2\sqrt{3}$ = _____

35) $8\sqrt{2} \times 2\sqrt{2}$ = _____

36) $6\sqrt{3} - \sqrt{12}$ = _____

Answers – Chapter 9

Multiplication Property of Exponents

1) 2^3
2) 5^4
3) 3^4
4) 4^4
5) 7^6
6) 2^5
7) 5^7
8) $2x^2$
9) x^5
10) x^8
11) x^6

12) $36x^2$
13) $4x^4$
14) $3x^3$
15) $64x^{12}$
16) $2x^4$
17) $3x^5$
18) $2x^3$
19) $25x^8$
20) $4x^3y$
21) $3x^8y^2$
22) x^5y^7

23) $8x^5y^4$
24) $36x^5y^4$
25) $21x^6y^8$
26) $63x^3y^8$
27) $28x^4y^7$
28) $24x^7y^6$
29) $3x^4y^9$
30) $4x^5y^4$
31) $20x^6y^9$
32) $560x^{11}y^4$

Division Property of Exponents

1) $\frac{1}{2}$
2) 2^2
3) 5^4
4) $\frac{1}{3^4}$
5) $\frac{1}{x^2}$
6) $\frac{1}{3^2}$
7) 5^5
8) $\frac{1}{25}$

9) 3
10) $\frac{1}{2x^2}$
11) $\frac{3}{2x^2}$
12) $\frac{6}{7x^3}$
13) $\frac{4x^3}{3y^8}$
14) $\frac{5y^2}{x^5}$
15) $\frac{2x^3}{7}$

16) $\frac{4y^8}{x}$
17) $\frac{4}{5x^3y^9}$
18) $\frac{6}{5x^4}$
19) $\frac{16}{9x^4y}$
20) $\frac{1}{4}$
21) $\frac{2}{9x^3}$

Powers of Products and Quotients

1) 4^4
2) 6^6
3) 2^{16}
4) 4^{10}
5) 3^{15}
6) 5^{18}
7) 2^{10}
8) 2^{12}

9) $121x^{10}$
10) $256x^8y^{16}$
11) $8x^{12}y^{12}$
12) $9x^4y^4$
13) $81x^{16}y^{12}$
14) $4x^{12}y^{16}$
15) $1,728x^{12}$
16) $8x^{45}$

17) $125x^{30}y^9$
18) $16x^{12}$
19) $225x^8$
20) $100x^{22}y^6$
21) $81x^{14}y^{10}$
22) $1,024x^{20}y^{30}$

Effortless
Math
Education

23) $144x^2y^6$

24) $\frac{25}{x^2}$

25) x^6y^6

26) $\frac{25}{x^{10}}$

27) $\frac{x^4}{y^4}$

28) x^4y^2

29) $\frac{4y^8}{x^4}$

30) $\frac{125}{y^6}$

Zero and Negative Exponents

1) 1

2) $\frac{1}{4}$

3) 0

4) 1

5) $\frac{1}{8}$

6) $\frac{1}{64}$

7) $\frac{1}{16}$

8) $\frac{1}{100}$

9) $\frac{1}{9}$

10) $\frac{1}{9}$

11) $\frac{1}{49}$

12) $\frac{1}{81}$

13) $\frac{1}{36}$

14) $\frac{1}{125}$

15) $\frac{1}{22}$

16) $\frac{1}{16}$

17) $\frac{1}{25}$

18) $\frac{1}{35}$

19) $\frac{1}{64}$

20) $\frac{1}{216}$

21) $\frac{1}{243}$

22) $\frac{1}{625}$

23) $\frac{1}{8}$

24) $\frac{1}{27}$

25) $\frac{1}{343}$

26) $\frac{1}{1,296}$

27) $\frac{1}{512}$

28) $\frac{1}{81}$

29) $\frac{1}{1,000}$

30) $\frac{1}{1,000,000,000}$

31) 2

32) 4

33) 9

34) $\frac{9}{4}$

35) 125

36) $\frac{16}{9}$

37) $\frac{25}{4}$

38) 256

39) $\frac{125}{8}$

40) $\frac{49}{9}$

41) $\frac{216}{125}$

42) $\frac{81}{16}$

Negative Exponents and Negative Bases

1) $-\frac{1}{6}$

2) $-\frac{1}{25}$

3) $-\frac{1}{16}$

4) $-\frac{1}{x^3}$

5) $\frac{2}{x}$

6) $-\frac{4}{x^3}$

7) $-\frac{12}{x^5}$

8) $-\frac{5}{x^2y^3}$

9) $\frac{20}{x^4y}$

10) $\frac{14}{a^6b^7}$

11) $-\frac{12x^2}{y^3}$

12) $-25x^6$

13) $-2xa^4$

14) 9

15) $\dfrac{16}{9}$

16) $-9a^7b^2$

17) $-5x^4$

18) $-\dfrac{b^2}{a^3}$

19) $-5x^3$

20) $-\dfrac{7bc^4}{9}$

21) $7a^4b^2$

22) $-\dfrac{p^3}{2n^2}$

23) $-\dfrac{4ac^2}{3b^2}$

24) $\dfrac{4c^2}{9a^2}$

25) $-\dfrac{27y^3z^3}{125x^3}$

26) $\dfrac{2}{b^2c^3}$

27) x^2

28) $-27x^{12}$

29) x^{12}

Scientific Notation

1) 1.13×10^{-1}

2) 2×10^{-2}

3) 2.5×10^0

4) 2×10^1

5) 6×10^1

6) 4×10^{-3}

7) 7.8×10^1

8) 1.6×10^3

9) 1.45×10^3

10) 9.1×10^4

11) 2×10^6

12) 6×10^{-7}

13) 3.54×10^5

14) 3.25×10^{-4}

15) 2.3×10^{-4}

16) 5.6×10^7

17) 2.1×10^4

18) 7.8×10^7

19) 2.2×10^{-6}

20) 1.2×10^{-4}

21) 0.3

22) 0.05

23) $1,200$

24) 0.0002

25) 0.015

26) $4,000$

27) $900,000$

28) $11,200$

29) 0.00003

30) 0.000083

Radicals

1) 0

2) 1

3) 2

4) 4

5) 3

6) 5

7) 7

8) 6

9) 8

10) 9

11) 11

12) 15

13) 12

14) 10

15) 16

16) 17

17) 18

18) 20

19) 30

20) 23

21) $3\sqrt{10}$

22) 13

23) 14

24) 19

25) 8

26) 40

27) 4

28) 6

29) 5

30) 8

31) $2\sqrt{2}$

32) $2\sqrt{8}$

33) $2\sqrt{5}$

34) 18

35) 32

36) $4\sqrt{3}$

Effortless Math Education

Chapter 10:
Polynomials

Math Topics that you'll learn in this Chapter:

- ✓ Simplifying Polynomials
- ✓ Adding and Subtracting Polynomials
- ✓ Multiplying Monomials
- ✓ Multiplying and Dividing Monomials
- ✓ Multiplying a Polynomial and a Monomial
- ✓ Multiplying Binomials
- ✓ Factoring Trinomials

Simplifying Polynomials

✎ *Simplify each expression.*

1) $5(2x - 10) =$

2) $2x(4x - 2) =$

3) $4x(5x - 3) =$

4) $3x(7x + 3) =$

5) $4x(8x - 4) =$

6) $5x(5x + 4) =$

7) $(2x - 3)(x - 4) =$

8) $(x - 5)(3x + 4) =$

9) $(x - 5)(x - 3) =$

10) $(3x + 8)(3x - 8) =$

11) $(3x - 8)(3x - 4) =$

12) $3x^2 + 3x^2 - 2x^3 =$

13) $2x - x^2 + 6x^3 + 4 =$

14) $5x + 2x^2 - 9x^3 =$

15) $7x^2 + 5x^4 - 2x^3 =$

16) $-3x^2 + 5x^3 + 6x^4 =$

17) $-8x^2 + 2x^3 - 10x^4 + 5x =$

18) $11 - 6x^2 + 5x^2 - 12x^3 + 22 =$

19) $2x^2 - 2x + 3x^3 + 12x - 22x =$

20) $11 - 4x^2 + 3x^2 - 7x^3 + 3 =$

21) $2x^5 - x^3 + 8x^2 - 2x^5 =$

22) $(2x^3 - 1) + (3x^3 - 2x^3) =$

23) $3(4x^4 - 4x^3 - 5x^4) =$

24) $-5(x^6 + 10) - 8(14 - x^6) =$

25) $3x^2 - 5x^3 - x + 10 - 2x^2 =$

26) $11 - 3x^2 + 2x^2 - 5x^3 + 7 =$

27) $(8x^2 - 3x) - (5x - 5 - 8x^2) =$

28) $3x^2 - 5x^3 - x(2x^2 + 4x) =$

29) $4x + 8x^3 - 4 - 3(x^3 - 2) =$

30) $12 + 2x^2 - (8x^3 - x^2 + 6x^3) =$

31) $-2(x^4 + 6) - 5(10 + x^4) =$

32) $(8x^3 - 2x) - (5x - 2x^3) =$

Adding and Subtracting Polynomials

✎ *Add or subtract expressions.*

1) $(-x^2 - 2) + (2x^2 + 1) =$

2) $(2x^2 + 3) - (3 - 4x^2) =$

3) $(2x^3 + 3x^2) - (x^3 + 8) =$

4) $(4x^3 - x^2) + (3x^2 - 5x) =$

5) $(7x^3 + 9x) - (3x^3 + 2) =$

6) $(2x^3 - 2) + (2x^3 + 2) =$

7) $(4x^3 + 5) - (7 - 2x^3) =$

8) $(4x^2 + 2x^3) - (2x^3 + 5) =$

9) $(4x^2 - x) + (3x - 5x^2) =$

10) $(7x + 9) - (3x + 9) =$

11) $(4x^4 - 2x) - (6x - 2x^4) =$

12) $(12x - 4x^3) - (8x^3 + 6x) =$

13) $(2x^3 - 8x^2) - (5x^2 - 3x) =$

14) $(2x^2 - 6) + (9x^2 - 4x^3) =$

15) $(4x^3 + 3x^4) - (x^4 - 5x^3) =$

16) $(-2x^3 - 2x) + (6x - 2x^3) =$

17) $(2x - 4x^4) - (8x^4 + 3x) =$

18) $(2x - 8x^2) - (5x^4 - 3x^2) =$

19) $(2x^3 - 6) + (9x^3 - 4x^2) =$

20) $(4x^3 + 3x^4) - (x^4 - 5x^3) =$

21) $(-2x^2 + 10x^4 + x^3) + (4x^3 + 3x^4 + 8x^2) =$

22) $(3x^2 - 6x^5 - 2x) - (-2x^2 - 6x^5 + 2x) =$

23) $(5x + 9x^3 - 3x^5) + (8x^3 + 3x^5 - 2x) =$

24) $(3x^5 - 2x^4 - 4x) - (4x^2 + 10x^4 - 3x) =$

25) $(13x^2 - 6x^5 - 2x) - (-10x^2 - 11x^5 + 9x) =$

26) $(-12x^4 + 10x^5 + 2x^3) + (14x^3 + 23x^5 + 8x^4) =$

Multiplying Monomials

✏️ *Simplify each expression.*

1) $4u^9 \times (-2u^3) =$

2) $(-2p^7) \times (-3p^2) =$

3) $3xy^2z^3 \times 2z^2 =$

4) $5u^5t \times 3ut^2 =$

5) $(-9a^6) \times (-5a^2b^4) =$

6) $-2a^3b^2 \times 4a^2b =$

7) $2xy^2 \times x^2y^3 =$

8) $3p^2q^4 \times (-2pq^3) =$

9) $4s^5t^2 \times 4st^3 =$

10) $(-6x^3y^2) \times 3x^2y =$

11) $2xy^2z \times 4z^2 =$

12) $4xy \times x^2y =$

13) $4pq^3 \times (-2p^4q) =$

14) $8s^4t^2 \times st^5 =$

15) $12p^3 \times (-3p^4) =$

16) $(-4p^2q^3r) \times 6pq^2r^3 =$

17) $(-8a^4) \times -12a^6b =$

18) $3u^4v^2 \times (-7u^2v^3) =$

19) $4u^3 \times (-2u) =$

20) $-6xy^2 \times 3x^2y =$

21) $12y^2z^3 \times (-y^2z) =$

22) $5a^2bc^2 \times 2abc^2 =$

23) $(-7p^3q^5) \times (-4p^2q^3) =$

24) $4u^5v^2 \times (-8u^3v^2) =$

25) $12y^3z^4 \times (-y^6z) =$

26) $(-4pq^5r^3) \times 6p^2q^4r =$

27) $5ab^4c^2 \times 2a^5bc^2 =$

28) $2x^4yz^3 \times 3x^2y^4z^2 =$

Multiplying and Dividing Monomials

✎ *Simplify each expression.*

1) $(2x^2)(x^3) =$

2) $(3x^4)(2x^4) =$

3) $(6x^5)(2x^2) =$

4) $(4x^3)(3x^5) =$

5) $(15x^4)(3x^9) =$

6) $(2yx^2)(3y^2x^3) =$

7) $(2x^2y)(x^2y^3) =$

8) $(-2x^3y^4)(3x^3y^2) =$

9) $(-5x^3y^2)(-2x^4y^5) =$

10) $(9x^5y)(-3x^3y^3) =$

11) $(8x^7y^2)(6x^5y^4) =$

12) $(7x^4y^6)(4x^3y^4) =$

13) $(12x^2y^9)(7x^9y^{12}) =$

14) $(6x^2y^5)(5x^3y^2) =$

15) $(9x^2y^9)(4x^{10}y^9) =$

16) $(-10x^4y^8)(2x^9y^5) =$

17) $\dfrac{4x^2y^3}{xy^2} =$

18) $\dfrac{2x^4y^3}{2x^3y} =$

19) $\dfrac{8x^2y^2}{4xy} =$

20) $\dfrac{6x^3y^4}{2x^2y^3} =$

21) $\dfrac{12x^6y^8}{4x^4y^2} =$

22) $\dfrac{26x^9y^5}{2x^3y^4} =$

23) $\dfrac{80x^{12}y^9}{10x^6y^7} =$

24) $\dfrac{95x^{18}y^7}{5x^9y^2} =$

25) $\dfrac{200x^3y^8}{40x^3y^7} =$

26) $\dfrac{-15x^{17}y^{13}}{3x^6y^9} =$

27) $\dfrac{-64x^8y^{10}}{8x^3y^7} =$

bit.ly/2WHp4

Find more at

Multiplying a Polynomial and a Monomial

✎ *Find each product.*

1) $x(x + 3) =$

2) $8(2 - x) =$

3) $2x(2x + 1) =$

4) $x(-x + 3) =$

5) $3x(3x - 2) =$

6) $5(3x - 6y) =$

7) $8x(7x - 4) =$

8) $3x(9x + 2y) =$

9) $6x(x + 2y) =$

10) $9x(2x + 4y) =$

11) $12x(3x + 9) =$

12) $11x(2x - 11y) =$

13) $2x(6x - 6y) =$

14) $2x(3x - 6y + 3) =$

15) $5x(3x^2 + 2y^2) =$

16) $13x(4x + 8y) =$

17) $5(2x^2 - 9y^2) =$

18) $3x(-2x^2y + 3y) =$

19) $-2(2x^2 - 2xy + 2) =$

20) $3(x^2 - 4xy - 8) =$

21) $2x(2x^2 - 3xy + 2x) =$

22) $-x(-x^2 - 5x + 4xy) =$

23) $9(x^2 + xy - 8y^2) =$

24) $3x(2x^2 - 3x + 8) =$

25) $20(2x^2 - 8x - 5) =$

26) $x^2(-x^2 + 3x + 7) =$

27) $x^3(x^2 + 12 - 2x) =$

28) $6x^3(3x^2 - 2x + 2) =$

29) $8x^2(3x^2 - 5xy + 7y^2) =$

30) $2x^2(3x^2 - 5x + 12) =$

31) $2x^3(2x^2 + 5x - 4) =$

32) $5x(6x^2 - 5xy + 2y^2) =$

Multiplying Binomials

✍ *Find each product.*

1) $(x + 2)(x + 2) =$

2) $(x - 3)(x + 2) =$

3) $(x - 2)(x - 4) =$

4) $(x + 3)(x + 2) =$

5) $(x - 4)(x - 5) =$

6) $(x + 5)(x + 2) =$

7) $(x - 6)(x + 3) =$

8) $(x - 8)(x - 4) =$

9) $(x + 2)(x + 8) =$

10) $(x - 2)(x + 4) =$

11) $(x + 4)(x + 4) =$

12) $(x + 5)(x + 5) =$

13) $(x - 3)(x + 3) =$

14) $(x - 2)(x + 2) =$

15) $(x + 3)(x + 3) =$

16) $(x + 4)(x + 6) =$

17) $(x - 7)(x + 7) =$

18) $(x - 7)(x + 2) =$

19) $(2x + 2)(x + 3) =$

20) $(2x - 3)(2x + 4) =$

21) $(x - 8)(2x + 8) =$

22) $(x - 7)(x - 6) =$

23) $(x - 8)(x + 8) =$

24) $(3x - 2)(4x + 2) =$

25) $(2x - 5)(x + 7) =$

26) $(5x - 4)(3x + 3) =$

27) $(6x + 9)(4x + 9) =$

28) $(2x - 6)(5x + 6) =$

29) $(x + 4)(4x - 8) =$

30) $(6x - 4)(6x + 4) =$

31) $(3x + 3)(3x - 4) =$

32) $(x^2 + 2)(x^2 - 2) =$

Factoring Trinomials

✎ *Factor each trinomial.*

1) $x^2 + 8x + 15 =$

2) $x^2 - 5x + 6 =$

3) $x^2 + 6x + 8 =$

4) $x^2 - 6x + 8 =$

5) $x^2 - 8x + 16 =$

6) $x^2 - 7x + 12 =$

7) $x^2 + 11x + 18 =$

8) $x^2 + 2x - 24 =$

9) $x^2 + 4x - 12 =$

10) $x^2 - 10x + 9 =$

11) $x^2 + 5x - 14 =$

12) $x^2 - 6x - 27 =$

13) $x^2 - 11x - 42 =$

14) $x^2 + 22x + 121 =$

15) $6x^2 + x - 12 =$

16) $x^2 - 17x + 30 =$

17) $3x^2 + 11x - 4 =$

18) $10x^2 + 33x - 7 =$

19) $x^2 + 24x + 144 =$

20) $8x^2 + 10x - 3 =$

✎ *Solve each problem.*

21) The area of a rectangle is $x^2 + 2x - 24$. If the width of rectangle is $x - 4$, what is its length? _____

22) The area of a parallelogram is $8x^2 + 2x - 6$ and its height is $2x + 2$. What is the base of the parallelogram? _____

23) The area of a rectangle is $18x^2 + 9x - 2$. If the width of the rectangle is $6x - 1$, what is its length? _____

Answers – Chapter 10

Simplifying Polynomials

1) $10x - 50$
2) $8x^2 - 4x$
3) $20x^2 - 12x$
4) $21x^2 + 9x$
5) $32x^2 - 16x$
6) $25x^2 + 20x$
7) $2x^2 - 11x + 12$
8) $3x^2 - 11x - 20$
9) $x^2 - 8x + 15$
10) $9x^2 - 64$
11) $9x^2 - 36x + 32$
12) $-2x^3 + 6x^2$
13) $6x^3 - x^2 + 2x + 4$
14) $-9x^3 + 2x^2 + 5x$
15) $5x^4 - 2x^3 + 7x^2$
16) $6x^4 + 5x^3 - 3x^2$
17) $-10x^4 + 2x^3 - 8x^2 + 5x$
18) $-12x^3 - x^2 + 33$
19) $3x^3 + 2x^2 - 12x$
20) $-7x^3 - x^2 + 14$
21) $-x^3 + 8x^2$
22) $3x^3 - 1$
23) $-3x^4 - 12x^3$
24) $3x^6 - 162$
25) $-5x^3 + x^2 - x + 10$
26) $-5x^3 - x^2 + 18$
27) $16x^2 - 8x + 5$
28) $-7x^3 - x^2$
29) $5x^3 + 4x + 2$
30) $-14x^3 + 3x^2 + 12$
31) $-7x^4 - 62$
32) $10x^3 - 7x$

Adding and Subtracting Polynomials

1) $x^2 - 1$
2) $6x^2$
3) $x^3 + 3x^2 - 8$
4) $4x^3 + 2x^2 - 5x$
5) $4x^3 + 9x - 2$
6) $4x^3$
7) $6x^3 - 2$
8) $4x^2 - 5$
9) $-x^2 + 2x$
10) $4x$
11) $6x^4 - 8x$
12) $-12x^3 + 6x$
13) $2x^3 - 13x^2 + 3x$
14) $-4x^3 + 11x^2 - 6$
15) $2x^4 + 9x^3$
16) $-4x^3 + 4x$
17) $-12x^4 - x$
18) $-5x^4 - 5x^2 + 2x$
19) $11x^3 - 4x^2 - 6$
20) $2x^4 + 9x^3$
21) $13x^4 + 5x^3 + 6x^2$
22) $5x^2 - 4x$
23) $17x^3 + 3x$
24) $3x^5 - 12x^4 - 4x^2 - x$
25) $5x^5 + 23x^2 - 11x$
26) $33x^5 - 4x^4 + 16x^3$

Multiplying Monomials

1) $-8u^{12}$
2) $6p^9$
3) $6xy^2z^5$
4) $15u^6t^3$

Effortless
Math
Education

5) $45a^8b^4$

6) $-8a^5b^3$

7) $2x^3y^5$

8) $-6p^3q^7$

9) $16s^6t^5$

10) $-18x^5y^3$

11) $8xy^2z^3$

12) $4x^3y^2$

13) $-8p^5q^4$

14) $8s^5t^7$

15) $-36p^7$

16) $-24p^3q^5r^4$

17) $96a^{10}b$

18) $-21u^6v^5$

19) $-8u^4$

20) $-18x^3y^3$

21) $-12y^4z^4$

22) $10a^3b^2c^4$

23) $28p^5q^8$

24) $-32u^8v^4$

25) $-12y^9z^5$

26) $-24p^3q^9r^4$

27) $10a^6b^5c^4$

28) $6x^6y^5z^5$

Multiplying and Dividing Monomials

1) $2x^5$

2) $6x^8$

3) $12x^7$

4) $12x^8$

5) $45x^{13}$

6) $6x^5y^3$

7) $2x^4y^4$

8) $-6x^6y^6$

9) $10x^7y^7$

10) $-27x^8y^4$

11) $48x^{12}y^6$

12) $28x^7y^{10}$

13) $84x^{11}y^{21}$

14) $30x^5y^7$

15) $36x^{12}y^{18}$

16) $-20x^{13}y^{13}$

17) $4xy$

18) xy^2

19) $2xy$

20) $3xy$

21) $3x^2y^6$

22) $13x^6y$

23) $8x^6y^2$

24) $19x^9y^5$

25) $5y$

26) $-5x^{11}y^4$

27) $-8x^5y^3$

Multiplying a Polynomial and a Monomial

1) $x^2 + 3x$

2) $-8x + 16$

3) $4x^2 + 2x$

4) $-x^2 + 3x$

5) $9x^2 - 6x$

6) $15x - 30y$

7) $56x^2 - 32x$

8) $27x^2 + 6xy$

9) $6x^2 + 12xy$

10) $18x^2 + 36xy$

11) $36x^2 + 108x$

12) $22x^2 - 121xy$

13) $12x^2 - 12xy$

14) $6x^2 - 12xy + 6x$

15) $15x^3 + 10xy^2$

16) $52x^2 + 104xy$

17) $10x^2 - 45y^2$

18) $-6x^3y + 9xy$

19) $-4x^2 + 4xy - 4$

20) $3x^2 - 12xy - 24$

21) $4x^3 - 6x^2y + 4x^2$

22) $x^3 + 5x^2 - 4x^2y$

23) $9x^2 + 9xy - 72y^2$

24) $6x^3 - 9x^2 + 24x$

25) $40x^2 - 160x - 100$

26) $-x^4 + 3x^3 + 7x^2$

27) $x^5 - 2x^4 + 12x^3$

28) $18x^5 - 12x^4 + 12x^3$

29) $24x^4 - 40x^3y + 56x^2y^2$

30) $6x^4 - 10x^3 + 24x^2$

31) $4x^5 + 10x^4 - 8x^3$

32) $30x^3 - 25x^2y + 10xy^2$

Effortless

Math

Education

Multiplying Binomials

1) $x^2 + 4x + 4$

2) $x^2 - x - 6$

3) $x^2 - 6x + 8$

4) $x^2 + 5x + 6$

5) $x^2 - 9x + 20$

6) $x^2 + 7x + 10$

7) $x^2 - 3x - 18$

8) $x^2 - 12x + 32$

9) $x^2 + 10x + 16$

10) $x^2 + 2x - 8$

11) $x^2 + 8x + 16$

12) $x^2 + 10x + 25$

13) $x^2 - 9$

14) $x^2 - 4$

15) $x^2 + 6x + 9$

16) $x^2 + 10x + 24$

17) $x^2 - 49$

18) $x^2 - 5x - 14$

19) $2x^2 + 8x + 6$

20) $4x^2 + 2x - 12$

21) $2x^2 - 8x - 64$

22) $x^2 - 13x + 42$

23) $x^2 - 64$

24) $12x^2 - 2x - 4$

25) $2x^2 + 9x - 35$

26) $15x^2 + 3x - 12$

27) $24x^2 + 90x + 81$

28) $10x^2 - 18x - 36$

29) $4x^2 + 8x - 32$

30) $36x^2 - 16$

31) $9x^2 - 3x - 12$

32) $x^4 - 4$

Factoring Trinomials

1) $(x + 3)(x + 5)$

2) $(x - 2)(x - 3)$

3) $(x + 4)(x + 2)$

4) $(x - 2)(x - 4)$

5) $(x - 4)(x - 4)$

6) $(x - 3)(x - 4)$

7) $(x + 2)(x + 9)$

8) $(x + 6)(x - 4)$

9) $(x - 2)(x + 6)$

10) $(x - 1)(x - 9)$

11) $(x - 2)(x + 7)$

12) $(x - 9)(x + 3)$

13) $(x + 3)(x - 14)$

14) $(x + 11)(x + 11)$

15) $(2x + 3)(3x - 4)$

16) $(x - 15)(x - 2)$

17) $(3x - 1)(x + 4)$

18) $(5x - 1)(2x + 7)$

19) $(x + 12)(x + 12)$

20) $(4x - 1)(2x + 3)$

21) $(x + 6)$

22) $(4x - 3)$

23) $(3x + 2)$

Effortless

Math

Education

Chapter 11: Geometry and Solid Figures

Math Topics that you'll learn in this Chapter:

- ✓ The Pythagorean Theorem
- ✓ Complementary and Supplementary Angles
- ✓ Parallel lines and Transversals
- ✓ Triangles
- ✓ Special Right Triangles
- ✓ Polygons
- ✓ Circles
- ✓ Trapezoids
- ✓ Cubes
- ✓ Rectangle Prisms
- ✓ Cylinder

93

Pythagorean Theorem

✍ *Do the following lengths form a right triangle?*

1)
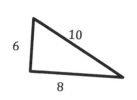

2)
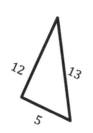

3)
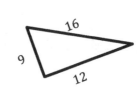

4)
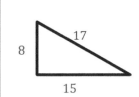

5)

6)
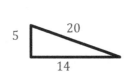

7)
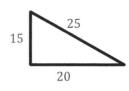

8)
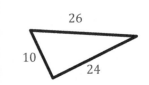

✍ *Find the missing side.*

9)
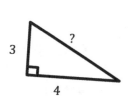

10)
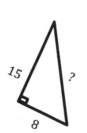

11)
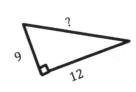

12)
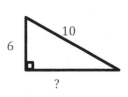

13)

14)

15)

16)
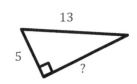

Complementary and Supplementary Angles

✏️ *Find the missing measurement in the pair of angles.*

1) $x =$ _____

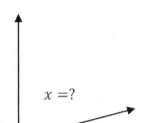

$x =?$

$20°$

2) $x =$ _____

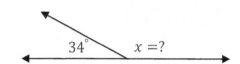

$34°$ $x =?$

3) **The measure of an angle is $58°$. What is the measure of its complementary angle?** _____

4) **The measure of an angle is $135°$. What is the measure of its supplementary angle?** _____

5) **Angles A and B are complementary. If $A = 3x - 8$ and $B = 5x + 10$, what is the measure of each angle?**

$A =$ _____ $B =$ _____

Parallel Lines and Transversals

✍ *Find the measure of each angle indicated.*

1)   ? = ____

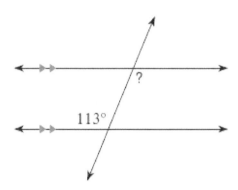

2)   ? = ____

✍ *In the following diagrams, solve for x.*

3) $x =$ ____

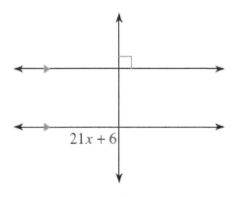

4) $x =$ ____

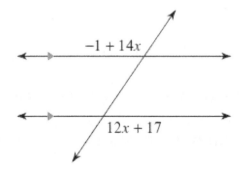

Triangles

✏️ *Find the measure of the unknown angle in each triangle.*

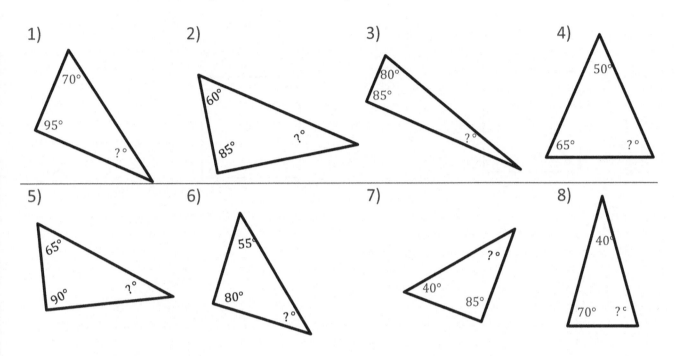

1) 70° 95° ?°

2) 60° 85° ?°

3) 80° 85° ?°

4) 50° 65° ?°

5) 65° 90° ?°

6) 55° 80° ?°

7) ?° 40° 85°

8) 40° 70° ?°

✏️ *Find area of each triangle.*

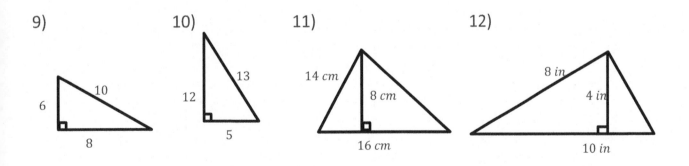

9) 6, 10, 8

10) 12, 13, 5

11) 14 cm, 8 cm, 16 cm

12) 8 in, 4 in, 10 in

Special Right Triangles

✎ *Find the value of x and y in each triangle.*

1) $x =$ ___ $y =$ ___

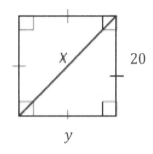

20

2) $x =$ ___ $y =$ ___

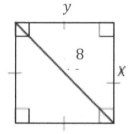

8

3) $x =$ ___ $y =$ ___

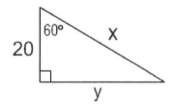

60°   X
20
y

4) $x =$ ___ $y =$ ___

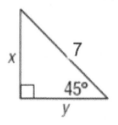

x   7
45°
y

5) $x =$ ___ $y =$ ___

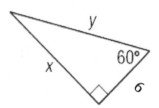

y
60°
x   6

6) $x =$ ___ $y =$ ___

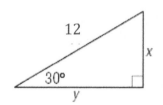

12   x
30°
y

Polygons

 Find the perimeter of each shape.

1)

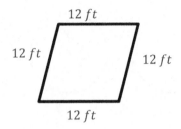

12 ft
12 ft   12 ft
12 ft

2)

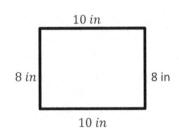

10 in
8 in   8 in
10 in

3)

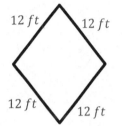

12 ft   12 ft
12 ft   12 ft

4) Square

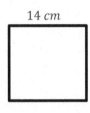

14 cm

5) Regular hexagon

5 m

6)

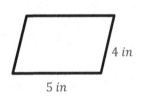

4.5 cm
5.5 cm
4 cm
5.5 cm
4.5 cm

7) Parallelogram

4 in
5 in

8) Square

6 m

 Find the area of each shape.

9) Parallelogram

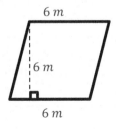

6 m
6 m
6 m

10) Rectangle

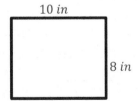

10 in
8 in

11) Rectangle

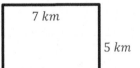

7 km
5 km

12) Square

7 in

Circles

✎ *Find the Circumference of each circle.* (π = 3.14)

1) ____   2) ____   3) ____   4) ____   5) ____   6) ____

7) ____   8) ____   9) ____   10) ____   11) ____   12) ____

✎ *Complete the table below.* (π = 3.14)

	Radius	Diameter	Circumference	Area
Circle 1	2 inches	4 inches	12.56 inches	12.56 square inches
Circle 2		8 meters		
Circle 3				113.04 square ft
Circle 4			50.24 miles	
Circle 5		9 km		
Circle 6	7 cm			
Circle 7		10 feet		
Circle 8				615.44 square meters
Circle 9			81.64 inches	
Circle 10	12 feet			

Trapezoids

📐 **Find the area of each trapezoid.**

1)   2)   3)   4)

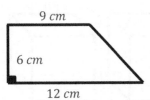   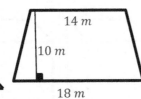   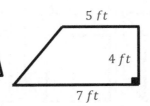   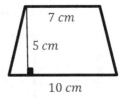

5)   6)   7)   8)

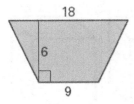   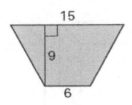   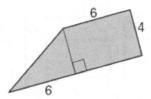   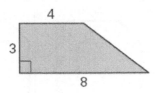

📐 **Solve.**

9) A trapezoid has an area of $60\ cm^2$ and its height is $6\ cm$ and one base is $8\ cm$. What is the other base length? _____

10) If a trapezoid has an area of $65\ ft^2$ and the lengths of the bases are $12\ ft$ and $14\ ft$, find the height. _____

11) If a trapezoid has an area of $180\ m^2$ and its height is $12\ m$ and one base is $20\ m$, find the other base length. _____

12) The area of a trapezoid is $625\ ft^2$ and its height is $25\ ft$. If one base of the trapezoid is $15\ ft$, what is the other base length?

_____

Cubes

✎ *Find the volume of each cube.*

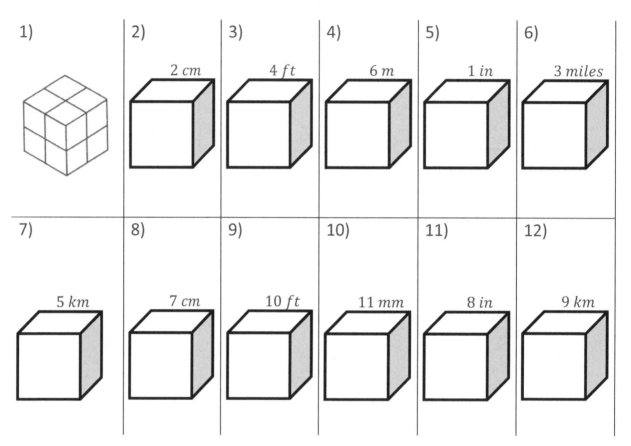

1)

2) 2 cm

3) 4 ft

4) 6 m

5) 1 in

6) 3 miles

7) 5 km

8) 7 cm

9) 10 ft

10) 11 mm

11) 8 in

12) 9 km

✎ *Find the surface area of each cube.*

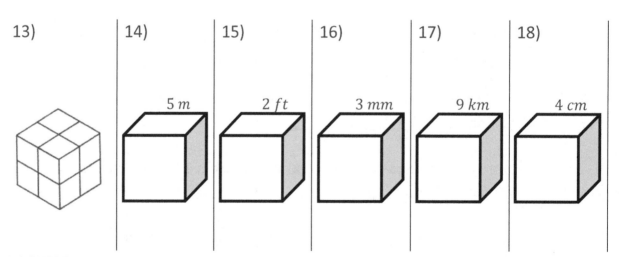

13)

14) 5 m

15) 2 ft

16) 3 mm

17) 9 km

18) 4 cm

Rectangular Prism

✍ **Find the volume of each Rectangular Prism.**

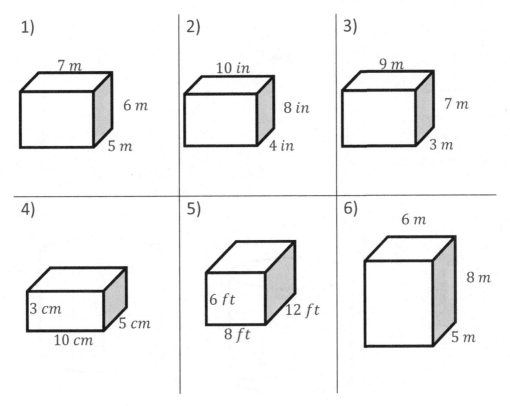

1) 7 m, 6 m, 5 m

2) 10 in, 8 in, 4 in

3) 9 m, 7 m, 3 m

4) 3 cm, 5 cm, 10 cm

5) 6 ft, 12 ft, 8 ft

6) 6 m, 8 m, 5 m

✍ **Find the surface area of each Rectangular Prism.**

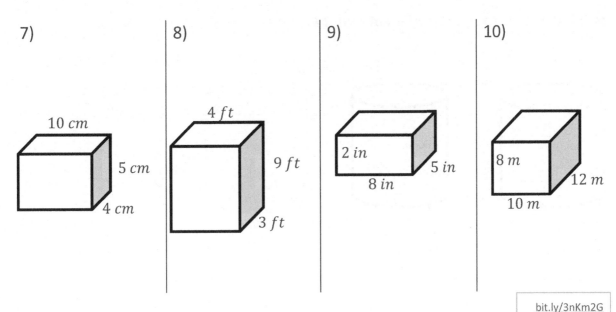

7) 10 cm, 5 cm, 4 cm

8) 4 ft, 9 ft, 3 ft

9) 2 in, 8 in, 5 in

10) 8 m, 10 m, 12 m

Cylinder

✎ *Find the volume of each Cylinder. Round your answer to the nearest tenth.* ($\pi = 3.14$)

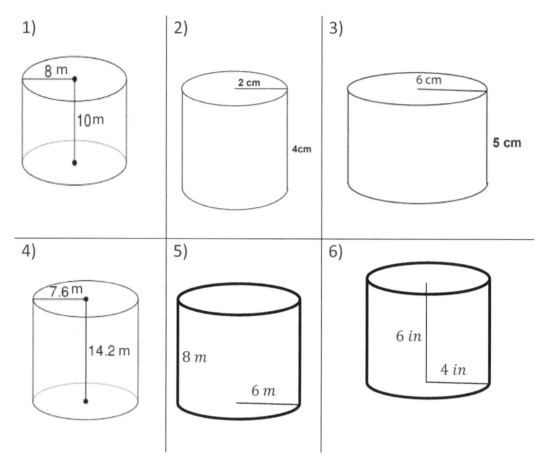

1) 8 m 10m

2) 2 cm 4cm

3) 6 cm 5 cm

4) 7.6 m 14.2 m

5) 8 m 6 m

6) 6 in 4 in

✎ *Find the surface area of each Cylinder.* ($\pi = 3.14$)

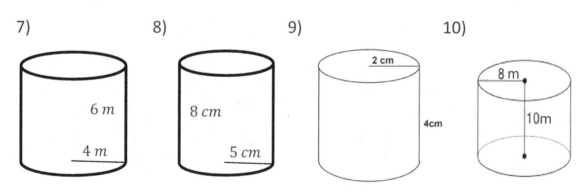

7) 6 m 4 m

8) 8 cm 5 cm

9) 2 cm 4cm

10) 8 m 10m

Answers – Chapter 11

Pythagorean Theorem

1) Yes	7) Yes	13) 5
2) Yes	8) Yes	14) 30
3) No	9) 5	15) 30
4) Yes	10) 17	16) 12
5) No	11) 15	
6) No	12) 8	

Complementary and Supplementary Angles

1) $70°$

2) $146°$

3) $32°$

4) $45°$

5) $A = 25°, B = 65°$

Parallel lines and Transversals

1) $111°$

2) $113°$

3) 4

4) 9

Triangles

1) $15°$	5) $25°$	9) 24 *square unites*
2) $35°$	6) $45°$	10) 30 *square unites*
3) $15°$	7) $55°$	11) 64 *square centimeters*
4) $65°$	8) $70°$	12) 20 *square inches*

Special Right Triangles

1) $x = 20\sqrt{2}$ $y = 20$

2) $x = 4\sqrt{2}$ $y = 4\sqrt{2}$

3) $x = 40$ $y = 20\sqrt{3}$

4) $x = \frac{7\sqrt{2}}{2}$ $y = \frac{7\sqrt{2}}{2}$

5) $x = 6\sqrt{3}$ $y = 12$

6) $x = 6$ $y = 6\sqrt{3}$

Polygons

1) $48\,ft$	6) $20\,cm$	10) $80\,in^2$
2) $36\,in$	7) $18\,in$	11) $35\,km^2$
3) $48\,ft$	8) $24\,m$	12) $49\,in^2$
4) $56\,cm$	9) $36\,m^2$	
5) $30\,m$		

Circles

1) $43.96\,in$

2) $75.36\,cm$

3) $87.92\,ft$

4) $81.64\,m$

5) $113.04\,cm$

6) $94.2\,miles$

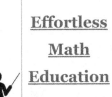

Effortless

Math

Education

7) 119.32 *in*   9) 157 *m*   11)   219.8 *in*
8) 138.16 *ft*   10) 175.84 *m*   12)   314 *ft*

	Radius	Diameter	Circumference	Area
Circle 1	2 inches	4 inches	12.56 inches	12.56 square inches
Circle 2	4 meters	8 meters	25.12 meters	50.24 square meters
Circle 3	6 ft	12 ft	37.68	113.04 square ft
Circle 4	8 miles	16 miles	50.24 miles	200.96 square miles
Circle 5	4.5 km	9 km	28.26 km	63.585 square km
Circle 6	7 cm	14 cm	43.96 cm	153.86 square cm
Circle 7	5 feet	10 feet	31.4 feet	78.5 square feet
Circle 8	14 m	28 m	87.92 m	615.44 square meters
Circle 9	13 in	26 in	81.64 inches	530.66 square inches
Circle 10	12 feet	24 feet	75.36 feet	452.16 square feet

Trapezoids

1) 63 cm^2 5) 81   10) 5 ft
2) 160 m^2 6) 94.5   11) 10 m
3) 24 ft^2 7) 36   12) 35 ft
4) 42.5 cm^2 8) 18
                          9) 12 cm

Cubes

1) 8 *square units*   7) 125 km^3 13) 24 *square units*
2) 8 cm^3 8) 343 cm^3 14) 150 m^2
3) 64 ft^3 9) 1,000 ft^3 15) 24 ft^2
4) 216 m^3 10) 1,331 mm^3 16) 54 mm^2
5) 1 in^3 11) 512 in^3 17) 486 km^2
6) 27 $miles^3$ 12) 729 km^3 18) 96 cm^2

Rectangular Prism

1) 210 m^3 5) 576 ft^3 9) 132 $in2$
2) 320 in^3 6) 240 m^3 10) 592 m^2
3) 189 m^3 7) 220 cm^2
4) 150 cm^3 8) 150 ft^2

**Effortless
Math
Education**

Cylinder

1) $2{,}009.6 \ m^3$
2) $50.24 \ cm^3$
3) $565.2 \ cm^3$
4) $2{,}575.4 \ m^3$

5) $904.3 \ m^3$
6) $301.4 \ in^3$
7) $251.2 \ m^2$
8) $408.2 \ cm^2$

9) $75.4 \ cm^2$
10) $904.3 \ m^2$

Effortless Math Education

Chapter 12: Statistics

Math Topics that you'll learn in this Chapter:

- ✓ Mean, Median,
- ✓ Mode and Range
- ✓ Pie Graph
- ✓ Probability Problems
- ✓ Permutations and Combinations

109

Mean and Median

✍ Find Mean and Median of the Given Data.

1) 8, 12, 5, 3, 2

2) 3, 6, 3, 7, 4, 13

3) 13, 5, 1, 7, 9

4) 6, 4, 2, 7, 3, 2

5) 6, 5, 7, 5, 7, 1, 11

6) 6, 1, 4, 4, 9, 2, 16

7) 12, 4, 1, 5, 9, 7, 7, 19

8) 18, 9, 5, 4, 9, 6, 12

9) 28, 25, 15, 16, 32, 44, 71

10) 10, 5, 1, 5, 4, 5, 8, 10

11) 18, 15, 30, 64, 42, 11

12) 44, 33, 56, 78, 41, 84

✍ Solve.

13) In a javelin throw competition, five athletics score $56, 58, 63, 57$ and 61 meters. What are their Mean and Median? _____

14) Eva went to shop and bought 3 apples, 5 peaches, 8 bananas, 1 pineapple and 3 melons. What are the Mean and Median of her purchase? _____

15) Bob has 12 black pen, 14 red pen, 15 green pens, 24 blue pens and 3 boxes of yellow pens. If the Mean and Median of the number of pens for each color are 16 and 15 respectively, what is the number of yellow pens in each box? _____

Mode and Range

✍ *Find Mode and Rage of the Given Data.*

1) $8, 2, 5, 9, 1, 2$

Mode: _____   Range: _____

2) $6, 6, 2, 3, 6, 3, 9, 12$

Mode: _____   Range: _____

3) $4, 4, 3, 9, 7, 9, 4, 6, 4$

Mode: _____   Range: _____

4) $12, 9, 2, 9, 3, 2, 9, 5$

Mode: _____   Range: _____

5) $9, 5, 9, 5, 8, 9, 8$

Mode: _____   Range: _____

6) $0, 1, 4, 10, 9, 2, 9, 1, 5, 1$

Mode: _____   Range: _____

7) $6, 5, 6, 9, 7, 7, 5, 4, 3, 5$

Mode: _____   Range: _____

8) $7, 5, 4, 9, 6, 7, 7, 5, 2$

Mode: _____   Range: _____

9) $2, 2, 5, 6, 2, 4, 7, 6, 4, 9$

Mode: _____   Range: _____

10) $7, 5, 2, 5, 4, 5, 8, 10$

Mode: _____   Range: _____

11) $4, 1, 5, 2, 2, 12, 18, 2$

Mode: _____   Range: _____

12) $6, 3, 5, 9, 6, 6, 3, 12$

Mode: _____   Range: _____

✍ *Solve.*

13) A stationery sold 12 pencils, 36 red pens, 44 blue pens, 12 notebooks, 18 erasers, 34 rulers and 32 color pencils. What are the Mode and Range for the stationery sells?

Mode: _____   Range: _____

14) In an English test, eight students score $14, 13, 17, 11, 19, 20, 14$ and 15. What are their Mode and Range? _____

15) What is the range of the first 6 even numbers greater than 11? _____

Pie Graph

The circle graph below shows all Jason's expenses for last month. Jason spent $300 on his bills last month.

Answer following questions based on the Pie graph.

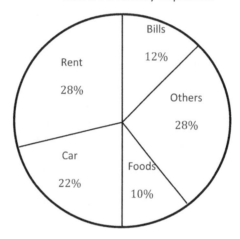

Jason's monthly expenses

1- How much did Jason spend on his car last month? _____

2- How much did Jason spend for foods last month? _____

3- How much did Jason spend on his rent last month? _____

4- What fraction is Jason's expenses for his bills and Car out of his total

expenses last month? _____

5- How much was Jason's total expenses last month? _____

Probability Problems

✎ *Solve.*

1) A number is chosen at random from **1** to **10**. Find the probability of selecting number **4** or smaller numbers. _____

2) Bag A contains **9** red marbles and **3** green marbles. Bag B contains **9** black marbles and **6** orange marbles. What is the probability of selecting a green marble at random from bag A? What is the probability of selecting a black marble at random from Bag B? _____ _____

3) A number is chosen at random from **1** to **50**. What is the probability of selecting multiples of **10**. _____

4) A card is chosen from a well-shuffled deck of **52** cards. What is the probability that the card will be a king OR a queen? (The deck includes **13** of each suit clubs, diamonds, hearts, and spades) _____

5) A number is chosen at random from **1** to **10**. What is the probability of selecting a multiple of **3**?_____

A spinner, numbered 1–8, is spun once. What is the probability of spinning...

6) an EVEN number? _____   7) a multiple of 3? _____

8) a PRIME number? _____   9) number 9? _____

bit.ly/3phwk1p

Find more at

Combinations and Permutations

✍ *Calculate the value of each.*

1) $4! = $ ____

2) $4! \times 3! = $ ____

3) $5! = $ ____

4) $6! + 3! = $ ____

5) $7! = $ ____

6) $8! = $ ____

7) $4! + 4! = $ ____

8) $4! - 3! = $ ____

✍ *Solve each word problems.*

9) Susan is baking cookies. She uses sugar, flour, butter, and eggs. How many different orders of ingredients can she try? _____

10) Jason is planning for his vacation. He wants to go to museum, watch a movie, go to the beach, and play volleyball. How many different ways of ordering are there for him? _____

11) How many 5-digit numbers can be named using the digits $1, 2, 3, 4$, and 5 without repetition? _____

12) In how many ways can 5 boys be arranged in a straight line? _____

13) In how many ways can 4 athletes be arranged in a straight line? _____

14) A professor is going to arrange her 7 students in a straight line. In how many ways can she do this? _____

15) How many code symbols can be formed with the letters for the word WHITE? _____

16) In how many ways a team of 8 basketball players can to choose a captain and co-captain? _____

Answers – Chapter 12

Mean and Median

1) Mean: 6, Median: 5
2) Mean: 6, Median: 5
3) Mean: 7, Median: 7
4) Mean: 4, Median: 3.5
5) Mean: 6, Median: 6

6) Mean: 6, Median: 4
7) Mean: 8, Median: 7
8) Mean: 9, Median: 9
9) Mean: 33, Median: 28
10) Mean: 6, Median: 5

11) Mean: 30, Median: 24
12) Mean: 56, Median: 50
13) Mean: 59, Median: 58
14) Mean: 4, Median: 3
15) 5

Mode and Range

1) Mode: 2, Range: 8
2) Mode: 6, Range: 10
3) Mode: 4, Range: 6
4) Mode: 9, Range: 10
5) Mode: 9, Range: 4

6) Mode: 1, Range: 10
7) Mode: 5, Range: 6
8) Mode: 7, Range: 7
9) Mode: 2, Range: 7
10) Mode: 5, Range: 8

11) Mode: 2, Range: 17
12) Mode: 6, Range: 9
13) Mode: 12, Range: 32
14) Mode: 14, Range: 9
15) 10

Pie Graph

1) $550
2) $250
3) $700

4) $\frac{17}{50}$
5) $2,500

Probability Problems

1) $\frac{2}{5}$
2) $\frac{1}{4}, \frac{3}{5}$
3) $\frac{1}{10}$

4) $\frac{2}{13}$
5) $\frac{3}{10}$
6) $\frac{1}{2}$

7) $\frac{1}{4}$
8) $\frac{1}{2}$
9) 0

Combinations and Permutations

1) 24
2) 144
3) 120
4) 726
5) 5,040
6) 40,320

7) 48
8) 18
9) 24
10) 24
11) 120
12) 120

13) 24
14) 5,040
15) 120
16) 56

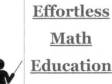

**Effortless
Math
Education**

Chapter 13: Functions Operations

Math Topics that you'll learn in this Chapter:

- ✓ Function Notation and Evaluation
- ✓ Adding and Subtracting Functions
- ✓ Multiplying and Dividing Functions
- ✓ Composition of Functions

Function Notation and Evaluation

✏️ *Evaluate each function.*

1) $f(x) = x - 3$, find $f(-2)$

_____

2) $g(x) = x + 5$, find $g(6)$

_____

3) $h(x) = x + 8$, find $h(2)$

_____

4) $f(x) = -x - 7$, find $f(5)$

_____

5) $f(x) = 2x - 7$, find $f(-1)$

_____

6) $w(x) = -2 - 4x$, find $w(5)$

_____

7) $g(n) = 6n - 3$, find $g(-2)$

_____

8) $h(x) = -8x + 12$, find $h(3)$

_____

9) $k(n) = 14 - 3n$, find $k(3)$

_____

10) $g(x) = 4x - 4$, find $g(-2)$

_____

11) $k(n) = 8n - 7$, find $k(4)$

_____

12) $w(n) = -2n + 14$, find $w(5)$

_____

13) $h(x) = 5x - 18$, find $h(8)$

_____

14) $g(n) = 2n^2 + 2$, find $g(5)$

_____

15) $f(x) = 3x^2 - 13$, find $f(2)$

_____

16) $g(n) = 5n^2 + 7$, find $g(-3)$

_____

17) $h(n) = 5n^2 - 10$, find $h(4)$

_____

18) $g(x) = -3x^2 - 6x$, find $g(2)$

_____

19) $k(n) = 4n^3 + n$, find $k(-5)$

_____

20) $f(x) = -3x + 10$, find $f(3x)$

_____

21) $k(a) = 4a + 9$, find $k(a - 1)$

_____

22) $h(x) = 8x + 4$, find $h(5x)$

_____

Adding and Subtracting Functions

✎ *Perform the indicated operation.*

1) $f(x) = x + 4$

    $g(x) = 2x + 5$

    Find $(f - g)(2)$

    _____

2) $g(x) = x - 2$

    $f(x) = -x - 6$

    Find $(g - f)(-2)$

    _____

3) $h(t) = 4t + 4$

    $g(t) = 3t + 2$

    Find $(h + g)(-1)$

    _____

4) $g(a) = 5a - 7$

    $f(a) = a^2 + 3$

    Find $(g + f)(2)$

    _____

5) $g(x) = 4x - 5$

    $f(x) = 6x^2 + 5$

    Find $(g - f)(-2)$

    _____

6) $h(x) = x^2 + 3$

    $g(x) = -4x + 1$

    Find $(h + g)(4)$

    _____

7) $f(x) = -3x - 9$

    $g(x) = x^2 + 5$

    Find $(f - g)(6)$

    _____

8) $h(n) = -4n^2 + 9$

    $g(n) = 5n + 6$

    Find $(h - g)(5)$

    _____

9) $g(x) = 4x^2 - 3x - 1$

    $f(x) = 6x + 10$

    Find $(g - f)(a)$

    _____

10) $g(t) = -6t - 7$

    $f(t) = -t^2 + 3t + 15$

    Find $(g + f)(t)$

    _____

Multiplying and Dividing Functions

✎ *Perform the indicated operation.*

1) $g(x) = x + 6$

    $f(x) = x + 4$

    Find $(g.f)(2)$

    _____

2) $f(x) = 3x$

    $h(x) = -x + 5$

    Find $(f.h)(-2)$

    _____

3) $g(a) = a + 5$

    $h(a) = 2a - 4$

    Find $(g.h)(4)$

    _____

4) $f(x) = 3x + 2$

    $h(x) = 2x - 3$

    Find $\left(\dfrac{f}{h}\right)(2)$

    _____

5) $f(x) = a^2 - 2$

    $g(x) = -4 + 3a$

    Find $\left(\dfrac{f}{g}\right)(2)$

    _____

6) $g(a) = 4a + 6$

    $f(a) = 2a - 8$

    Find $\left(\dfrac{g}{f}\right)(3)$

    _____

7) $g(t) = t^2 + 6$

    $h(t) = 2t - 3$

    Find $(g.h)(-3)$

    _____

8) $g(x) = x^2 + 3x + 4$

    $h(x) = 2x + 6$

    Find $(g.h)(2)$

    _____

9) $g(a) = 2a^2 - 5a + 1$

    $f(a) = 2a^3 - 6$

    Find $\left(\dfrac{g}{f}\right)(4)$

    _____

10) $g(x) = -3x^2 + 4 - 2x$

    $f(x) = x^2 - 5$

    Find $(g.f)(3)$

    _____

Composition of Functions

✍ **Using $f(x) = x + 6$ and $g(x) = 3x$, find:**

1) $f(g(1)) = $ ___

2) $f(g(-1)) = $ ___

3) $g(f(-3)) = $ ___

4) $g(f(4)) = $ ___

5) $f(g(2)) = $ ___

6) $g(f(3)) = $ ___

✍ **Using $f(x) = 2x + 5$ and $g(x) = x - 2$, find:**

7) $g(f(2)) = $ ___

8) $g(f(-2)) = $ ___

9) $f(g(5)) = $ ___

10) $f(f(4)) = $ ___

11) $g(f(3)) = $ ___

12) $g(f(-3)) = $ ___

✍ **Using $f(x) = 4x - 2$ and $g(x) = x - 5$, find:**

13) $g(f(-2)) = $ ___

14) $f(f(4)) = $ ___

15) $f(g(5)) = $ ___

16) $f(f(3)) = $ ___

17) $g(f(-3)) = $ ___

18) $g(g(6)) = $ ___

✍ **Using $f(x) = 6x + 2$ and $g(x) = 2x - 3$, find:**

19) $f(g(-3)) = $ ___

20) $g(f(5)) = $ ___

21) $f(g(4)) = $ ___

22) $f(f(3)) = $ ___

bit.ly/2WHBkAg

Find more at

Answers – Chapter 13

Function Notation and Evaluation

1) -5
2) 11
3) 10
4) -12
5) -9
6) -22
7) -15
8) -12

9) 5
10) -12
11) 25
12) 4
13) 22
14) 52
15) -1
16) 52

17) 70
18) -24
19) -505
20) $-9x + 10$
21) $4a + 5$
22) $40x + 4$

Adding and Subtracting Functions

1) -3
2) 0
3) -1
4) 10

5) -42
6) 4
7) -68
8) -122

9) $4a^2 - 9a - 11$
10) $-t^2 - 3t + 8$

Multiplying and Dividing Functions

1) 48
2) -42
3) 36
4) 8

5) 1
6) -9
7) -135
8) 140

9) $\frac{13}{122}$
10) -116

Composition of Functions

1) $f\big(g(1)\big) = 9$
2) $f\big(g(-1)\big) = 3$
3) $g\big(f(-3)\big) = 9$
4) $g\big(f(4)\big) = 30$
5) $f\big(g(2)\big) = 12$
6) $g\big(f(3)\big) = 27$
7) $g\big(f(2)\big) = 7$
8) $g\big(f(-2)\big) = -1$

9) $f\big(g(5)\big) = 11$
10) $f\big(f(4)\big) = 31$
11) $g\big(f(3)\big) = 9$
12) $g\big(f(-3)\big) = -3$
13) $g\big(f(-2)\big) = -15$
14) $f\big(f(4)\big) = 54$
15) $f\big(g(5)\big) = -2$
16) $f\big(f(3)\big) = 38$

17) $g\big(f(-3)\big) = -19$
18) $g\big(g(6)\big) = -4$
19) $f\big(g(-3)\big) = -52$
20) $g\big(f(5)\big) = 61$
21) $f\big(g(4)\big) = 32$
22) $f\big(f(3)\big) = 122$

Effortless
Math
Education

Time to Test

Time to refine your skill with a practice examination

In this section, there are two complete HiSET Mathematics Tests. Take a REAL HiSET Mathematics test to simulate the test day experience. After you've finished, score your test using the answer key.

Before You Start

- You'll need a pencil, a calculator, and a timer to take the test.
- It's okay to guess. You won't lose any points if you're wrong. So be sure to answer every question.
- After you've finished the test, review the answer key to see where you went wrong.
- **Calculators are permitted for HiSET Math Test.**
- Use the answer sheet provided to record your answers.
- The HiSET Mathematics test contains a formula sheet, which displays formulas relating to geometric measurement and certain algebra concepts. Formulas are provided to test- takers so that they may focus on application, rather than the memorization, of formulas.
- For each multiple-choice question, there are five possible answers. Choose which one is best.

Good Luck!

HiSET Mathematics

Practice Test 1

2022

Total number of questions: 55

Total time (Calculator): 90 Minutes

Calculators are permitted for HiSET Math Test.

125

HiSET Mathematics Practice Tests Answer Sheet

Remove (or photocopy) this answer sheet and use it to complete the practice test.

HiSET Mathematics Practice Test 1 Answer Sheet

1	Ⓐ Ⓑ Ⓒ Ⓓ Ⓔ	21	Ⓐ Ⓑ Ⓒ Ⓓ Ⓔ	41	Ⓐ Ⓑ Ⓒ Ⓓ Ⓔ
2	Ⓐ Ⓑ Ⓒ Ⓓ Ⓔ	22	Ⓐ Ⓑ Ⓒ Ⓓ Ⓔ	42	Ⓐ Ⓑ Ⓒ Ⓓ Ⓔ
3	Ⓐ Ⓑ Ⓒ Ⓓ Ⓔ	23	Ⓐ Ⓑ Ⓒ Ⓓ Ⓔ	43	Ⓐ Ⓑ Ⓒ Ⓓ Ⓔ
4	Ⓐ Ⓑ Ⓒ Ⓓ Ⓔ	24	Ⓐ Ⓑ Ⓒ Ⓓ Ⓔ	44	Ⓐ Ⓑ Ⓒ Ⓓ Ⓔ
5	Ⓐ Ⓑ Ⓒ Ⓓ Ⓔ	25	Ⓐ Ⓑ Ⓒ Ⓓ Ⓔ	45	Ⓐ Ⓑ Ⓒ Ⓓ Ⓔ
6	Ⓐ Ⓑ Ⓒ Ⓓ Ⓔ	26	Ⓐ Ⓑ Ⓒ Ⓓ Ⓔ	46	Ⓐ Ⓑ Ⓒ Ⓓ Ⓔ
7	Ⓐ Ⓑ Ⓒ Ⓓ Ⓔ	27	Ⓐ Ⓑ Ⓒ Ⓓ Ⓔ	47	Ⓐ Ⓑ Ⓒ Ⓓ Ⓔ
8	Ⓐ Ⓑ Ⓒ Ⓓ Ⓔ	28	Ⓐ Ⓑ Ⓒ Ⓓ Ⓔ	48	Ⓐ Ⓑ Ⓒ Ⓓ Ⓔ
9	Ⓐ Ⓑ Ⓒ Ⓓ Ⓔ	29	Ⓐ Ⓑ Ⓒ Ⓓ Ⓔ	49	Ⓐ Ⓑ Ⓒ Ⓓ Ⓔ
10	Ⓐ Ⓑ Ⓒ Ⓓ Ⓔ	30	Ⓐ Ⓑ Ⓒ Ⓓ Ⓔ	50	Ⓐ Ⓑ Ⓒ Ⓓ Ⓔ
11	Ⓐ Ⓑ Ⓒ Ⓓ Ⓔ	31	Ⓐ Ⓑ Ⓒ Ⓓ Ⓔ	51	Ⓐ Ⓑ Ⓒ Ⓓ Ⓔ
12	Ⓐ Ⓑ Ⓒ Ⓓ Ⓔ	32	Ⓐ Ⓑ Ⓒ Ⓓ Ⓔ	52	Ⓐ Ⓑ Ⓒ Ⓓ Ⓔ
13	Ⓐ Ⓑ Ⓒ Ⓓ Ⓔ	33	Ⓐ Ⓑ Ⓒ Ⓓ Ⓔ	53	Ⓐ Ⓑ Ⓒ Ⓓ Ⓔ
14	Ⓐ Ⓑ Ⓒ Ⓓ Ⓔ	34	Ⓐ Ⓑ Ⓒ Ⓓ Ⓔ	54	Ⓐ Ⓑ Ⓒ Ⓓ Ⓔ
15	Ⓐ Ⓑ Ⓒ Ⓓ Ⓔ	35	Ⓐ Ⓑ Ⓒ Ⓓ Ⓔ	55	Ⓐ Ⓑ Ⓒ Ⓓ Ⓔ
16	Ⓐ Ⓑ Ⓒ Ⓓ Ⓔ	36	Ⓐ Ⓑ Ⓒ Ⓓ Ⓔ		
17	Ⓐ Ⓑ Ⓒ Ⓓ Ⓔ	37	Ⓐ Ⓑ Ⓒ Ⓓ Ⓔ		
18	Ⓐ Ⓑ Ⓒ Ⓓ Ⓔ	38	Ⓐ Ⓑ Ⓒ Ⓓ Ⓔ		
19	Ⓐ Ⓑ Ⓒ Ⓓ Ⓔ	39	Ⓐ Ⓑ Ⓒ Ⓓ Ⓔ		
20	Ⓐ Ⓑ Ⓒ Ⓓ Ⓔ	40	Ⓐ Ⓑ Ⓒ Ⓓ Ⓔ		

Formula Sheet

Perimeter / Circumference

Rectangle

$Perimeter = 2(length) + 2(width)$

Circle

$Circumference = 2\pi(radius)$

Area

Circle

$Area = \pi(radius)^2$

Triangle

$Area = \frac{1}{2}(base)(height)$

Parallelogram

$Area = (base)(height)$

Trapezoid

$Area = \frac{1}{2}(base_1 + base_2)(height)$

Volume

Prism/Cylinder

$Volume = (area\ of\ the\ base)(height)$

Pyramid/Cone

$Volume = \frac{1}{3}(area\ of\ the\ base)(height)$

Sphere

$Volume = \frac{4}{3}\pi(radius)^3$

Length

1 foot = 12 inches

1 yard = 3 feet

1 mile = 5,280 feet

1 meter = 1,000 millimeters

1 meter = 100 centimeters

1 kilometer = 1,000 meters

1 mile ≈ 1.6 kilometers

1 inch = 2.54 centimeters

1 foot ≈ 0.3 meter

Capacity / Volume

1 cup = 8 fluid ounces

1 pint = 2 cups

1 quart = 2 pints

1 gallon = 4 quarts

1 gallon = 231 cubic inches

1 liter = 1,000 milliliters

1 liter ≈ 0.264 gallon

Weight

1 pound = 16 ounces

1 ton = 2,000 pounds

1 gram = 1,000 milligrams

1 kilogram = 1,000 grams

1 kilogram ≈ 2.2 pounds

1 ounce ≈ 28.3 grams

1) What is the length of AB in the following figure if AE = 4, CD = 6 and AC = 12?

   A. 3.8

   B. 4.8

   C. 7.2

   D. 24

   E. 48

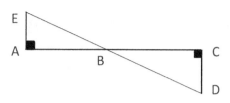

2) If the area of the following trapezoid is 126 *cm*, what is the perimeter of the trapezoid? (Figure not drawn to scale.)

   A. 12 *cm*

   B. 13 *cm*

   C. 32 *cm*

   D. 46 *cm*

   E. 55 *cm*

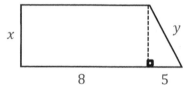

3) If 5 *inches* on a map represents an actual distance of 100 feet, then, what actual distance does 18 inches on the map represent?

   A. 18

   B. 20

   C. 100

   D. 250

   E. 360

4) Which of the following lists shows the fractions in order from least to greatest?

$$\frac{3}{4}, \frac{2}{7}, \frac{3}{8}, \frac{5}{11}$$

   A. $\frac{3}{8}, \frac{2}{7}, \frac{3}{4}, \frac{5}{11}$

   B. $\frac{3}{8}, \frac{2}{7}, \frac{5}{11}, \frac{3}{4}$

   C. $\frac{2}{7}, \frac{5}{11}, \frac{3}{8}, \frac{3}{4}$

   D. $\frac{2}{7}, \frac{3}{8}, \frac{5}{11}, \frac{3}{4}$

   E. $\frac{5}{11}, \frac{3}{4}, \frac{3}{8}, \frac{2}{7}$

5) The following graph shows the mark of seven students in mathematics. What is the mean (average) of the marks?

A. 15

B. 14.5

C. 14

D. 13.5

E. 13

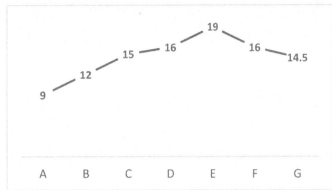

Questions 6 to 8 are based on the following data

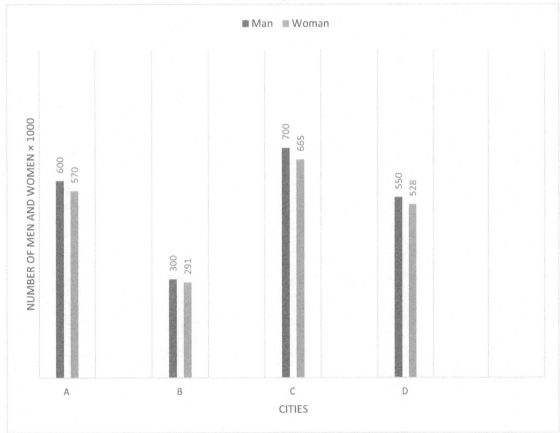

6) What's the maximum ratio of woman to man in the four cities?

A. 0.98

B. 0.97

C. 0.96

D. 0.95

E. 0.94

7) What's the ratio of percentage of men in city A to percentage of women in city C?

    A. 0.85

    B. 0.9

    C. 0.95

    D. 1

    E. 1.05

8) How many women should be added to city D until the ratio of women to men will be 1.2?

    A. 120

    B. 123

    C. 128

    D. 132

    E. 160

9) What is the value of 6^4?

    A. 6

    B. 24

    C. 36

    D. 216

    E. 1,296

10) How many $\frac{1}{5}$ pound paperback books together weigh 50 pounds?

    A. 25

    B. 50

    C. 150

    D. 200

    E. 250

11) What is the volume of the following square pyramid?

    A. $100\ m^3$

    B. $120\ m^3$

    C. $144\ m^3$

    D. $480\ m^3$

    E. $1,440\ m^3$

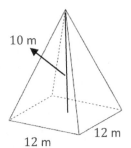

10 m
12 m
12 m

12) The surface area of a cylinder is $150\pi\ cm^2$. If its height is $10\ cm$, what is the radius of the cylinder?

   A. $20\ cm$

   B. $15\ cm$

   C. $13\ cm$

   D. $11\ cm$

   E. $5\ cm$

13) In the following shape, the area of the circle is 16π. What is the area of the square?

   A. 4

   B. 8

   C. 16

   D. 32

   E. 64

14) List A consists of the numbers $\{1, 3, 8, 10, 15\}$, and list B consists of the numbers $\{4, 6, 12, 14, 17\}$. If the two lists are combined, what is the median of the combined list?

   A. 9

   B. 10

   C. 12

   D. 15

   E. 17

15) What's the area of the non-shaded part of the following figure?

   A. 236

   B. 192

   C. 152

   D. 42

   E. 40

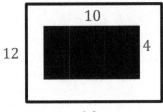

16) In the triangle below, if the measure of angle A is 37 degrees, then what is the value of y? (figure is NOT drawn to scale)

A. 37

B. 62

C. 70

D. 78

E. 86

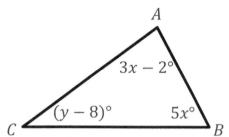

Questions 17 to 19 are based on the following data

Types of air pollutions in 10 cities of a country

Type of Pollution	Number of Cities									
A	■	■	■	■	■	■				
B	■	■	■							
C	■	■	■	■						
D	■	■	■	■	■	■	■	■	■	
E	■	■	■		■	■	■	■		
	1	2	3	4	5	6	7	8	9	10

17) If a is the mean (average) of the number of cities in each pollution type category, b is the mode, and c is the median of the number of cities in each pollution type category, then which of the following must be true?

A. $a < b < c$

B. $b < a < c$

C. $b < c < b$

D. $a = c$

E. $b < c = a$

18) What percent of cities are in the type of pollution A, C, and D respectively?

A. 60%, 40%, 90%

B. 40%, 90%, 60%

C. 40%, 60%, 90%

D. 30%, 40%, 90%

E. 30%, 40%, 60%

19) How many cities should be added to type of pollutions B until the ratio of cities in type of pollution B to cities in type of pollution E will be 0.625?

    A. 2

    B. 3

    C. 4

    D. 5

    E. 6

20) There are only red and blue cards in a box. The probability of choosing a red card in the box at random is one third. If there are 246 blue cards, how many cards are in the box?

    A. 123

    B. 246

    C. 308

    D. 328

    E. 369

21) $\frac{1}{6b^2} + \frac{1}{6b} = \frac{1}{b^2}$, then $b = ?$

    A. $-\frac{15}{16}$

    B. $-\frac{16}{15}$

    C. 5

    D. 6

    E. 8

22) In the diagram below, circle A represents the set of all odd numbers, circle B represents the set of all negative numbers, and circle C represents the set of all multiples of 5. Which number could be replaced with y?

    A. 0

    B. 5

    C. -5

    D. 10

    E. -10

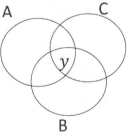

23) Which of the following graphs represents the compound inequality?

$$-2 \le 2x - 4 < 2?$$

A.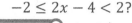
-6 -5 -4 -3 -2 -1 0 1 2 3 4 5 6

B.
-6 -5 -4 -3 -2 -1 0 1 2 3 4 5 6

C.
-6 -5 -4 -3 -2 -1 0 1 2 3 4 5 6

D.
-6 -5 -4 -3 -2 -1 0 1 2 3 4 5 6

E.
-6 -5 -4 -3 -2 -1 0 1 2 3 4 5 6

24) A basket contains 20 balls and the average weight of each of these balls is 25 g. The five heaviest balls have an average weight of 40 g each. If we remove the five heaviest balls from the basket, what is the average weight of the remaining balls?

A. 10

B. 20

C. 30

D. 35

E. 40

25) In a stadium the ratio of home fans to visiting fans in a crowd is $5:7$. Which of the following could be the total number of fans in the stadium?

A. 12,324

B. 42,326

C. 44,566

D. 66,812

E. 69,752

26) What is the perimeter of a square in centimeters that has an area of 595.36 cm^2?

A. 97.6

B. 96.2

C. 95.7

D. 92.6

E. 90.3

27) A bread recipe calls for $2\frac{2}{3}$ cups of flour. If you only have $1\frac{5}{6}$ cups, how much more flour is needed?

A. 1

B. 2

C. $\frac{1}{2}$

D. $\frac{5}{6}$

E. $\frac{11}{6}$

28) If $x = \frac{1}{3}$ and $y = \frac{9}{21}$, then which is equal to $\frac{1}{x} \div \frac{y}{3}$?

A. $\frac{1}{7}$

B. $\frac{1}{3}$

C. $\frac{2}{3}$

D. $\frac{1}{21}$

E. 21

29) If Jim adds 100 stamps to his current stamp collection, the total number of stamps will be equal to $\frac{6}{5}$ the current number of stamps. If Jim adds 50% more stamps to the current collection, how many stamps will be in the collection?

A. 150

B. 300

C. 500

D. 600

E. 750

30) The sum of 8 numbers is greater than 240 and less than 320. Which of the following could be the average (arithmetic mean) of the numbers?

A. 25

B. 30

C. 35

D. 40

E. 45

31) In the following figure, point Q lies on line n, what is the value of y if $x = 35$?

A. 15

B. 25

C. 30

D. 35

E. 45

32) Triangle ABC is similar to triangle ADE. What is the length of side EC?

A. 4.5

B. 9

C. 18

D. 27

E. 36

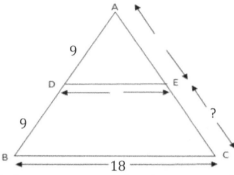

33) Ella (E) is 4 years older than her friend Ava (A) who is 3 years younger than her sister Sofia (S). If E, A and S denote their ages, which one of the following represents the given information?

A. $\begin{cases} E = A + 4 \\ S = A - 3 \end{cases}$

B. $\begin{cases} E = A + 4 \\ A = S + 3 \end{cases}$

C. $\begin{cases} A = E + 4 \\ S = A - 3 \end{cases}$

D. $\begin{cases} E = A + 4 \\ A = S - 3 \end{cases}$

E. $\begin{cases} E = A + 3 \\ S = A + 4 \end{cases}$

34) The length of a rectangle is 3 meters greater than 4 times its width. The perimeter of the rectangle is 36 meters. What is the area of the rectangle in meters?

A. 15

B. 35

C. 45

D. 55

E. 65

35) Find the value of x in the following diagram. (there are 2 supplementary angles in the diagram?

A. 23

B. 36

C. 47

D. 68

E. 90

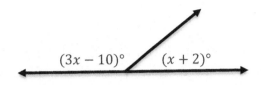

$(3x - 10)°$ $(x + 2)°$

36) The circle graph below shows all Mr. Green's expenses for last month. If he spent $660 on his car, how much did he spend for his rent?

A. $660

B. $700

C. $740

D. $780

E. $810

Mr. Green's monthly expenses

Bills 13%

Rent 27%

Others 28%

Car 22%

Foods 10%

37) What is the area of the shaded region if the diameter of the bigger circle is 12 inches and the diameter of the smaller circle is 8 inches?

A. $16\pi\ in^2$

B. $20\pi\ in^2$

C. $36\pi\ in^2$

D. $48\pi\ in^2$

E. $80\pi\ in^2$

38) In the rectangle below if $y > 5\ cm$ and the area of rectangle is $50\ cm^2$ and the perimeter of the rectangle is $30\ cm$, what is the value of x and y?

A. $x = 15,\ y = 10$

B. $x = 15,\ y = 5$

C. $x = 10,\ y = 15$

D. $x = 10,\ y = 5$

E. $x = 5,\ y = 10$

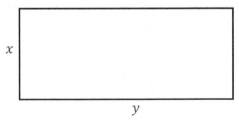

x

y

39) What is the value of x?

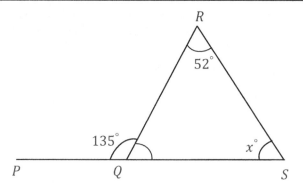

    A. 38

    B. 45

    C. 75

    D. 83

    E. 135

40) If x is directly proportional to the square of y, and $y = 2$ when $x = 12$, then when $x = 75$ $y = ?$

    A. $\frac{1}{5}$

    B. 1

    C. 5

    D. 12

    E. 25

41) Jack earns \$616 for his first 44 hours of work in a week and is then paid 1.5 times his regular hourly rate for any additional hours. This week, Jack needs \$826 to pay his rent, bills and other expenses. How many hours must he work to make enough money in this week?

    A. 40

    B. 43

    C. 48

    D. 54

    E. 62

42) What is 2.5% of 1,200?

    A. 900

    B. 600

    C. 300

    D. 60

    E. 30

43) If x is a real number, and if $x^3 + 18 = 130$, then x lies between which two consecutive integers?

    A. 1 and 2

    B. 2 and 3

    C. 3 and 4

    D. 4 and 5

    E. 5 and 6

44) Jack types 72 words per minute. How many words does he type in 15 seconds?

    A. 14

    B. 18

    C. 20

    D. 22

    E. 24

45) Which of the following is the same as: 0.000,000,000,000,042,121?

    A. 4.2121×10^{14}

    B. 4.2121×10^{13}

    C. 42.121×10^{-10}

    D. 42.121×10^{-13}

    E. 4.2121×10^{-14}

46) Which of the following is the largest?

    A. $|4 - 2|$

    B. $|2 - 4|$

    C. $|-2 - 4|$

    D. $|2 - 4| - |4 - 2|$

    E. $|2 - 4| + |4 - 2|$

47) A student gets 85% of a test with 40 questions. How many answers did the student solve correctly?

   A. 25

   B. 28

   C. 34

   D. 36

   E. 42

48) To buy a new computer, Emma borrowed $2,500 at 8% interest for 6 years. How much interest did she pay?

   A. $150

   B. $1,200

   C. $1,500

   D. $2,400

   E. $2,500

49) If n is an even integer that is less than -3.34, what is the greatest possible value of n?

   A. -1

   B. -2

   C. -3

   D. -4

   E. -5

50) Integer x is evenly divisible by 4. Which expression below is also evenly divisible by 4?

   A. $x + 1$

   B. $2x + 1$

   C. $2x + 4$

   D. $3x + 2$

   E. $4x + 1$

51) Sara has a box containing 5 blue balls, 8 red balls, and 3 green balls. If she removes one ball at random, what is the probability that it will not be blue?

   A. $\frac{1}{8}$

   B. $\frac{5}{16}$

   C. $\frac{5}{11}$

   D. $\frac{10}{11}$

   E. $\frac{11}{16}$

52) On the number line below, point M is located on line segment ON so that $OM = \frac{1}{3}MN$. What is the position of point M?

   A. -4.2

   B. -3.5

   C. -1.5

   D. 1.5

   E. 2.5

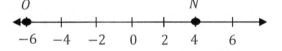

53) Jack rides 160 kilometers in 1 hour 20 minutes. At that rate, how many meters does he ride per minute?

   A. 1,000 meters

   B. 1,500 meters

   C. 1,600 meters

   D. 2,000 meters

   E. 2,500 meters

54) The sum of two consecutive integer is -13. If 2 is added to the smaller integer and 3 is subtract from the larger integer, what is the product of the two resulting integers?

   A. 5

   B. 9

   C. 18

   D. 28

   E. 45

55) A ladder leans against a wall forming a 60° angle between the ground and the ladder. If the bottom of the ladder is 30 feet away from the wall, how long is the ladder?

  A. 30 *feet*

  B. 40 *feet*

  C. 50 *feet*

  D. 60 *feet*

  E. 120 *feet*

End of HiSET Mathematics Practice Test 1

HiSET Mathematics

Practice Test 2

2022

Total number of questions: 55

Total time (Calculator): 90 Minutes

Calculators are permitted for HiSET Math Test.

143

HiSET Mathematics Practice Tests Answer Sheet

Remove (or photocopy) this answer sheet and use it to complete the practice test.

HiSET Mathematics Practice Test 2 Answer Sheet

1	Ⓐ Ⓑ Ⓒ Ⓓ Ⓔ	21 Ⓐ Ⓑ Ⓒ Ⓓ Ⓔ	41 Ⓐ Ⓑ Ⓒ Ⓓ Ⓔ
2	Ⓐ Ⓑ Ⓒ Ⓓ Ⓔ	22 Ⓐ Ⓑ Ⓒ Ⓓ Ⓔ	42 Ⓐ Ⓑ Ⓒ Ⓓ Ⓔ
3	Ⓐ Ⓑ Ⓒ Ⓓ Ⓔ	23 Ⓐ Ⓑ Ⓒ Ⓓ Ⓔ	43 Ⓐ Ⓑ Ⓒ Ⓓ Ⓔ
4	Ⓐ Ⓑ Ⓒ Ⓓ Ⓔ	24 Ⓐ Ⓑ Ⓒ Ⓓ Ⓔ	44 Ⓐ Ⓑ Ⓒ Ⓓ Ⓔ
5	Ⓐ Ⓑ Ⓒ Ⓓ Ⓔ	25 Ⓐ Ⓑ Ⓒ Ⓓ Ⓔ	45 Ⓐ Ⓑ Ⓒ Ⓓ Ⓔ
6	Ⓐ Ⓑ Ⓒ Ⓓ Ⓔ	26 Ⓐ Ⓑ Ⓒ Ⓓ Ⓔ	46 Ⓐ Ⓑ Ⓒ Ⓓ Ⓔ
7	Ⓐ Ⓑ Ⓒ Ⓓ Ⓔ	27 Ⓐ Ⓑ Ⓒ Ⓓ Ⓔ	47 Ⓐ Ⓑ Ⓒ Ⓓ Ⓔ
8	Ⓐ Ⓑ Ⓒ Ⓓ Ⓔ	28 Ⓐ Ⓑ Ⓒ Ⓓ Ⓔ	48 Ⓐ Ⓑ Ⓒ Ⓓ Ⓔ
9	Ⓐ Ⓑ Ⓒ Ⓓ Ⓔ	29 Ⓐ Ⓑ Ⓒ Ⓓ Ⓔ	49 Ⓐ Ⓑ Ⓒ Ⓓ Ⓔ
10	Ⓐ Ⓑ Ⓒ Ⓓ Ⓔ	30 Ⓐ Ⓑ Ⓒ Ⓓ Ⓔ	50 Ⓐ Ⓑ Ⓒ Ⓓ Ⓔ
11	Ⓐ Ⓑ Ⓒ Ⓓ Ⓔ	31 Ⓐ Ⓑ Ⓒ Ⓓ Ⓔ	51 Ⓐ Ⓑ Ⓒ Ⓓ Ⓔ
12	Ⓐ Ⓑ Ⓒ Ⓓ Ⓔ	32 Ⓐ Ⓑ Ⓒ Ⓓ Ⓔ	52 Ⓐ Ⓑ Ⓒ Ⓓ Ⓔ
13	Ⓐ Ⓑ Ⓒ Ⓓ Ⓔ	33 Ⓐ Ⓑ Ⓒ Ⓓ Ⓔ	53 Ⓐ Ⓑ Ⓒ Ⓓ Ⓔ
14	Ⓐ Ⓑ Ⓒ Ⓓ Ⓔ	34 Ⓐ Ⓑ Ⓒ Ⓓ Ⓔ	54 Ⓐ Ⓑ Ⓒ Ⓓ Ⓔ
15	Ⓐ Ⓑ Ⓒ Ⓓ Ⓔ	35 Ⓐ Ⓑ Ⓒ Ⓓ Ⓔ	55 Ⓐ Ⓑ Ⓒ Ⓓ Ⓔ
16	Ⓐ Ⓑ Ⓒ Ⓓ Ⓔ	36 Ⓐ Ⓑ Ⓒ Ⓓ Ⓔ	
17	Ⓐ Ⓑ Ⓒ Ⓓ Ⓔ	37 Ⓐ Ⓑ Ⓒ Ⓓ Ⓔ	
18	Ⓐ Ⓑ Ⓒ Ⓓ Ⓔ	38 Ⓐ Ⓑ Ⓒ Ⓓ Ⓔ	
19	Ⓐ Ⓑ Ⓒ Ⓓ Ⓔ	39 Ⓐ Ⓑ Ⓒ Ⓓ Ⓔ	
20	Ⓐ Ⓑ Ⓒ Ⓓ Ⓔ	40 Ⓐ Ⓑ Ⓒ Ⓓ Ⓔ	

Formula Sheet

Perimeter / Circumference

Rectangle

$Perimeter = 2(length) + 2(width)$

Circle

$Circumference = 2\pi(radius)$

Area

Circle

$Area = \pi(radius)^2$

Triangle

$Area = \dfrac{1}{2}(base)(height)$

Parallelogram

$Area = (base)(height)$

Trapezoid

$Area = \dfrac{1}{2}(base_1 + base_2)(height)$

Volume

Prism/Cylinder

$Volume = (area\ of\ the\ base)(height)$

Pyramid/Cone

$Volume = \dfrac{1}{3}(area\ of\ the\ base)(height)$

Sphere

$Volume = \dfrac{4}{3}\pi(radius)^3$

Length

1 foot = 12 inches

1 yard = 3 feet

1 mile = 5,280 feet

1 meter = 1,000 millimeters

1 meter = 100 centimeters

1 kilometer = 1,000 meters

1 mile ≈ 1.6 kilometers

1 inch = 2.54 centimeters

1 foot ≈ 0.3 meter

Capacity / Volume

1 cup = 8 fluid ounces

1 pint = 2 cups

1 quart = 2 pints

1 gallon = 4 quarts

1 gallon = 231 cubic inches

1 liter = 1,000 milliliters

1 liter ≈ 0.264 gallon

Weight

1 pound = 16 ounces

1 ton = 2,000 pounds

1 gram = 1,000 milligrams

1 kilogram = 1,000 grams

1 kilogram ≈ 2.2 pounds

1 ounce ≈ 28.3 grams

1) The capacity of a red box is 20% bigger than the capacity of a blue box. If the red box can hold 30 equal sized books, how many of the same books can the blue box hold?

    A. 9

    B. 15

    C. 21

    D. 25

    E. 30

2) Kim spent $35 for pants. This was $10 less than triple what she spent for a shirt. How much was the shirt?

    A. $11

    B. $13

    C. $15

    D. $17

    E. $21

3) What is the greatest integer less than $-\frac{32}{5}$?

    A. 0

    B. -2

    C. -4

    D. -6

    E. -7

4) The measure of the angles of a triangle are in the ratio $1:3:5$. What is the measure of the largest angle?

    A. $20°$

    B. $45°$

    C. $85°$

    D. $100°$

    E. $180°$

5) In the figure below, line A is parallel to line B. what is the value of x?

A. 28

B. 46

C. 50

D. 55

E. 65

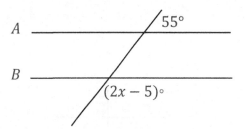

6) The mean of 50 test scores was calculated as 85. But it turned out that one of the scores was misread as 94 but it was 69. What is the mean?

A. 84.5

B. 87

C. 87.5

D. 88.5

E. 90.5

7) Which of the following answers represents the compound inequality?

8) $-4 \leq 4x - 8 < 16$?

A. $-2 \leq x \leq 8$

B. $-2 < x \leq 8$

C. $1 < x \leq 6$

D. $1 \leq x < 6$

E. $2 \leq x \leq 6$

8) In the following figure, $ABCD$ is a rectangle. If $a = \sqrt{3}$, and $b = 2a$, find the area of the shaded region. (the shaded region is a trapezoid)

A. $2\sqrt{3}$

B. $3\sqrt{3}$

C. $4\sqrt{3}$

D. $6\sqrt{3}$

E. $8\sqrt{3}$

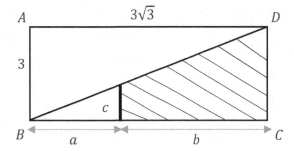

9) Which graph shows a non-proportional linear relationship between x and y?

A.

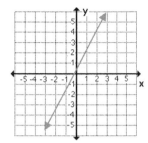

B.

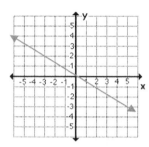

C.

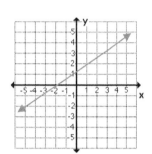

D.

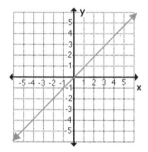

E.

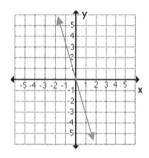

10) In the figure below, what is the value of x?

A. 8

B. 11

C. 15

D. 16

E. 32

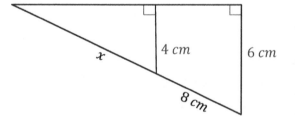

11) Anna opened an account with a deposit of $3,000. This account earns 5% simple interest annually. How many years will it take her to earn $600 on her $3,000 deposit?

    A. 2

    B. 4

    C. 5

    D. 6

    E. 8

12) Tom picked $2\frac{2}{5}$ baskets of apples, and Sam picked $1\frac{3}{4}$ baskets of apples. How many baskets total did they pick?

    A. $1\frac{2}{3}$

    B. $2\frac{1}{12}$

    C. $3\frac{20}{23}$

    D. $4\frac{3}{20}$

    E. $5\frac{1}{12}$

13) A list of consecutive integers begins with k and ends with n. If $n - k = 46$, how many integers are in the list?

    A. 23

    B. 38

    C. 46

    D. 47

    E. 58

14) A piece of paper that is $2\frac{3}{5}$ feet long is cut into 2 pieces of different lengths. The shorter piece has a length of x feet. Which inequality expresses all possible values of x?

    A. $x < 2\frac{1}{10}$

    B. $x > 2$

    C. $x < 2\frac{3}{5}$

    D. $x > 1\frac{3}{10}$

    E. $x < 1\frac{3}{10}$

15) In an academy, course grades range from 0 to 100. Anna took 5 courses and her mean course grade was 80. William took 8 courses. If both students have the same sum of course grades, what was William's mean?

   A. 50

   B. 65

   C. 70

   D. 80

   E. 85

16) The sum of the numbers x, y, and z is 69. The ratio of x to y is $1:3$ and the ratio of y to z is $2:5$. What is the value of y?

   A. 9.6

   B. 15

   C. 18

   D. 21.6

   E. 33

17) Which number line below shows the solution to the inequality $-1 < \frac{x}{3} < 2$?

   A.

   B.

   C.

   D.

   E.

18) The set S consists of all odd numbers greater than 5 and less than 30. What is the mean of the numbers in S.

   A. 11

   B. 13

   C. 17

   D. 18

   E. 23

19) If $\sqrt{2y} = \sqrt{5x}$ then $x = \cdots$

   A. $\frac{1}{6}y$

   B. $\frac{1}{5}y$

   C. $\frac{2}{5}y$

   D. $\frac{5}{2}y$

   E. $10y$

20) A line connects the midpoint of AB (point E), with point C in the square $ABCD$. Calculate the area of the acquired trapezoid shape if the square has a side of $4\ m$.

   A. $4\ cm^2$

   B. $12\ cm^2$

   C. $15\ cm^2$

   D. $18\ cm^2$

   E. $24\ cm^2$

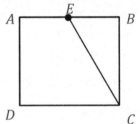

21) In a group of 45 student, 60% can't swim. How many students can swim?

   A. 13

   B. 18

   C. 22

   D. 23

   E. 35

22) $8,400 are distributed equally among 14 person. How much money will each person get?

   A. $400

   B. $450

   C. $584

   D. $600

   E. $800

23) A box contains 6 green sticks, 4 blue sticks, and 2 yellow sticks. Emma picks one without looking. What is the probability that the stick will be green?

A. $\frac{1}{2}$

B. $\frac{1}{3}$

C. $\frac{1}{4}$

D. $\frac{2}{5}$

E. $\frac{3}{2}$

24) The figure below, a square is inscribed in a circle. Calculate the shaded area in the figure below. Knowing that the radius of the circle is 6 cm. ($\pi = 3.14$)

A. $73.65\ cm^2$

B. $69.90\ cm^2$

C. $72.69\ cm^2$

D. $88.04\ cm^2$

E. $113.4\ cm^2$

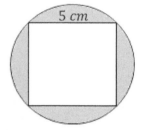

25) The price of a Chocolate was raised from $5.40 to $5.67. What was the percent increase in the price?

A. 4%

B. 5%

C. 6%

D. 8%

E. 10%

26) In a box of blue and black marbles, the ratio of blue marbles to black marbles is $4:3$. If the box contains 150 black marbles, how many blue marbles are there?

A. 100

B. 150

C. 200

D. 300

E. 600

27) $\frac{5}{8}$ of a number is 90. Find the number.

 A. 144

 B. 270

 C. 450

 D. 720

 E. 800

28) A juice mixture contains $\frac{5}{14}$ jar of cherry juice and $\frac{5}{70}$ jar of apple juice. How many jars of cherry juice per jar of apple juice does the mixture contain?

 A. 70

 B. 14

 C. 10

 D. 7

 E. 5

29) In the figure below, $LMNO$ and $JMPQ$ are squares. Point O is the center of the circle, and points L and N are on the circle. If the area of the square is 16 square centimeters, what is the area, in square centimeters, of the shaded part?
($\pi = 3.14$)

 A. 3

 B. 3.44

 C. 12

 D. 12.56

 E. 16

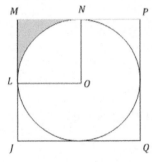

30) The set of possible values of n is $\{5, 3, 7\}$. What is the set of possible values of m if $2m = n + 5$?

 A. $\{2, 4, 7\}$

 B. $\{3, 2, 5\}$

 C. $\{4, 5, 8\}$

 D. $\{5, 4, 6\}$

 E. $\{6, 5, 8\}$

31) If $x = 25$, then which of the following equations are correct?

   A. $x + 10 = 40$

   B. $4x = 100$

   C. $3x = 70$

   D. $\frac{x}{2} = 12$

   E. $\frac{x}{3} = 8$

32) Jack scored a mean of 80 per test in his first 4 tests. In his 5th test, he scored 90. What was Jack's mean score for the 5 tests?

   A. 70

   B. 75

   C. 80

   D. 82

   E. 93

33) The volume of a cube is less than $64\ m^3$. Which of the following can be the cube's side?

   A. $2\ m$

   B. $4\ m$

   C. $8\ m$

   D. $10\ m$

   E. $11\ m$

34) What is the area of an isosceles right triangle that has one leg that measures $6\ cm$?

   A. $6\ cm^2$

   B. $12\ cm^2$

   C. $18\ cm^2$

   D. $24\ cm^2$

   E. $36\ cm^2$

35) If $0.00104 = \frac{104}{x}$, what is the value of x?

   A. 1,000

   B. 10,000

   C. 100,000

   D. 1,000,000

   E. 10,000,000

36) A bag is filled with numbered cards from 1 to 15 and picked on at random. What is the probability that the card picked is number 8?

   A. $\frac{8}{15}$

   B. $\frac{7}{15}$

   C. $\frac{5}{15}$

   D. $\frac{2}{15}$

   E. $\frac{1}{15}$

37) In the xy-plane, the point $(4,3)$ and $(3,2)$ are on line A. Which of the following points could also be on line A?

   A. $(5,7)$

   B. $(3,4)$

   C. $(-1,2)$

   D. $(-1,-2)$

   E. $(-7,-9)$

38) If $f(x)=2x^3+ 5x^2+ 2x$ and $g(x)= -2$, what is the value of $f(g(x))$?

   A. 36

   B. 32

   C. 24

   D. 4

   E. 0

39) What is the value of x in the figure below?

A. 32

B. 46

C. 54

D. 63

E. 76

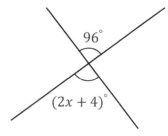

40) How many different two-digit numbers can be formed from the digits 6, 7, and 5, if the numbers must be even and no digit can be repeated?

A. 1

B. 2

C. 3

D. 4

E. 5

41) A rectangular concrete driveway is 25 feet long, 6 feet wide, and 24 inches thick. What is the volume of the concrete?

A. $300 \, ft^3$

B. $600 \, ft^3$

C. $660 \, ft^3$

D. $963 \, ft^3$

E. $1,800 \, ft^3$

42) If $\frac{2y}{x} - \frac{y}{3x} = \frac{(...)}{3x}$ and $x \neq 0$, what expression is represented by $(...)$?

A. $2y + 4$

B. $3y - 6$

C. $5y$

D. $6y$

E. $8y$

43) $200(3 + 0.01)^2 - 200 =$

    A. 201.55

    B. 361.08

    C. 702.88

    D. 1,612.02

    E. 1,812.02

44) If 360 kg of vegetables is packed in 90 boxes, how much vegetables will each box contain?

    A. 2.5 kg

    B. 3 kg

    C. 4 kg

    D. 6.5 kg

    E. 7 kg

45) Each number in a sequence is 4 more than twice the number that comes just before it. If 84 is a number in the sequence, what number comes just before it?

    A. 26

    B. 35

    C. 40

    D. 52

    E. 88

46) $[6 \times (-24) + 8] - (-4) + [4 \times 5] \div 2 = ?$

    A. 148

    B. 132

    C. -122

    D. -136

    E. -144

47) Solve for x: $2 + \frac{3x}{x-5} = \frac{3}{5-x}$?

    A. $\frac{4}{5}$

    B. $\frac{6}{5}$

    C. $\frac{7}{5}$

    D. $\frac{8}{5}$

    E. $\frac{9}{5}$

48) A rectangle has 14 cm wide and 5 cm length. What is the perimeter of this rectangle?

    A. 29 cm

    B. 38 cm

    C. 43 cm

    D. 49 cm

    E. 58 cm

49) What is the value of the following expression? $3\frac{1}{4} + 2\frac{4}{16} + 1\frac{3}{8} + 5\frac{1}{2}$

    A. $3\frac{10}{14}$

    B. $4\frac{1}{2}$

    C. $12\frac{4}{16}$

    D. $12\frac{3}{8}$

    E. $12\frac{4}{8}$

50) A certain insect has a mass of 85 milligrams. What is the insect's mass in grams?

    A. 0.085

    B. 0.08

    C. 0.85

    D. 8.5

    E. 85

51) Removing which of the following numbers will change the average of the numbers to 6?

$$1, 4, 5, 8, 11, 12$$

A. 1

B. 4

C. 5

D. 8

E. 11

52) If $m = 6$ and $n = -3$, what is the value of $\frac{5-9(3+n)}{3m-5(2-n)} =$?

A. $\frac{2}{7}$

B. $\frac{3}{7}$

C. $-\frac{4}{7}$

D. $\frac{5}{7}$

E. $-\frac{5}{7}$

53) Clara has 28 cookies. She is inviting 7 friends to a party. How many cookies will each friend get?

A. 2

B. 4

C. 7

D. 8

E. 21

54) How long will it take to receive $360 in investment of $240 at the rate of 10% simple interest?

A. 9 years

B. 15 years

C. 18 years

D. 21 years

E. 24 years

55) How many hours are there in 1,800 minutes?

    A. 20 hours

    B. 25 hours

    C. 30 hours

    D. 33 hours

    E. 60 hours

End of HiSET Mathematics Practice Test 2

HiSET Math Practice Tests Answer Keys

Now, it's time to review your results to see where you went wrong and what areas you need to improve.

	HiSET Practice Test 1						HiSET Practice Test 2					
1	B	21	C	41	D	1	D	21	B	41	A		
2	D	22	C	42	E	2	C	22	D	42	C		
3	E	23	D	43	D	3	E	23	A	43	D		
4	D	24	B	44	B	4	D	24	D	44	C		
5	B	25	A	45	E	5	E	25	B	45	C		
6	B	26	A	46	C	6	A	26	C	46	C		
7	E	27	D	47	C	7	D	27	A	47	C		
8	D	28	E	48	B	8	C	28	E	48	B		
9	E	29	E	49	D	9	C	29	B	49	D		
10	E	30	C	50	C	10	D	30	D	50	A		
11	D	31	B	51	E	11	B	31	B	51	E		
12	E	32	B	52	B	12	D	32	D	52	E		
13	E	33	D	53	D	13	D	33	A	53	B		
14	A	34	C	54	E	14	E	34	C	54	B		
15	C	35	C	55	D	15	A	35	C	55	C		
16	E	36	E			16	C	36	E				
17	D	37	E			17	D	37	D				
18	A	38	E			18	D	38	E				
19	A	39	D			19	C	39	B				
20	E	40	C			20	B	40	B				

HiSET Math Practice Tests

Answers and Explanations

HiSET Mathematics Practice Test 1 Answers

1) Choice B is correct

Two triangles ΔBAE and ΔBCD are similar. Then:

$\dfrac{AE}{CD} = \dfrac{AB}{BC} \to \dfrac{4}{6} = \dfrac{x}{12-x} \to 48 - 4x = 6x \to 10x = 48 \to x = 4.8$

2) Choice D is correct

The area of the trapezoid is:

$Area = \dfrac{1}{2}h(b_1 + b_2) \to 126 = \dfrac{1}{2}(x)(13 + 8) \to 126 = 10.5x \to x = 12$

$y = \sqrt{5^2 + 12^2} = \sqrt{25 + 144} = \sqrt{169} = 13$

The perimeter of the trapezoid is: $12 + 13 + 8 + 13 = 46$

3) Choice E is correct

First calculate the number of feet that 1 inch represents: $100\ ft \div 5\ in = 20\ ft/in$

Then multiply this by the total number of inches: $18\ in \times 20\ ft/in = 360\ ft$

4) Choice D is correct

Let's compare each fraction: $\dfrac{2}{7} < \dfrac{3}{8} < \dfrac{5}{11} < \dfrac{3}{4}$

Only choice D provides the right order.

5) Choice B is correct

Use the average formula:

$average\ (mean) = \dfrac{sum\ of\ terms}{number\ of\ terms} = \dfrac{9 + 12 + 15 + 16 + 19 + 16 + 14.5}{7} = 14.5$

6) Choice B is correct

Ratio of women to men in city A: $\dfrac{570}{600} = 0.95$

Ratio of women to men in city B: $\dfrac{291}{300} = 0.97$

Ratio of women to men in city C: $\dfrac{665}{700} = 0.95$

Ratio of women to men in city D: $\dfrac{528}{550} = 0.96$

Choice B is the maximum number.

7) Choice E is correct

Percentage of men in city $A = \dfrac{600}{1,170} \times 100 \approx 51.28\%$

Percentage of women in city $C = \frac{665}{1,365} \times 100 \approx 48.72\%$

Percentage of men in city A to percentage of women in city $C = \frac{51.28}{48.72} \approx 1.05$

(Notice that $\frac{51.28}{48.72}$ is bigger than 1 and only choice E is bigger than 1)

8) Choice D is correct

Let the number of women should be added to city D be x, then:

$\frac{528+x}{550} = 1.2 \rightarrow 528 + x = 550 \times 1.2 \rightarrow x = 132$

9) Choice E is correct

$6^4 = 6 \times 6 \times 6 \times 6 = 1,296$

10) Choice E is correct

If each book weighs $\frac{1}{5}$ pound, then 1 pound = 5 books. To find the number of books in 50 pounds, simply multiply this 5 by 50: $50 \times 5 = 250$

11) Choice D is correct

Use the volume of square pyramid formula.

$V = \frac{1}{3}a^2h \Rightarrow V = \frac{1}{3}(12\ m)^2 \times 10\ m \Rightarrow V = 480\ m^3$

12) Choice E is correct

Formula for the surface area of a cylinder is:

$SA = 2\pi r^2 + 2\pi rh \rightarrow 150\pi = 2\pi r^2 + 2\pi r(10) \rightarrow r^2 + 10r - 75 = 0$

Factor the expression and solve:

$r^2 + 10r - 75 = 0 \rightarrow (r + 15)(r - 5) = 0 \rightarrow r = 5\ or\ r = -15\ (unacceptable)$

13) Choice E is correct

The area of the circle is 16π, then, its diameter is 8.

Area of a circle $= \pi r^2 = 16\pi \rightarrow r^2 = 16 \rightarrow r = 4$

Radius of the circle is 4 and diameter is twice of it, 8.

One side of the square equals to the diameter of the circle. Then:

$Area\ of\ square = side \times side = 8 \times 8 = 64$

14) Choice A is correct

The median of a set of data is the value located in the middle of the data set. Combine the two sets provided, and organize them in increasing order:

$\{1, 3, 4, 6, 8, 10, 12, 14, 15, 17\}$

Since there are 10 numbers (an even number of items) in the resulting list, the median is the average of the two middle numbers. Median $= \frac{(8+10)}{2} = 9$

15) Choice C is correct

The area of the non-shaded region is equal to the area of the bigger rectangle subtracted by the area of smaller rectangle.

Area of the bigger rectangle $= 12 \times 16 = 192$

Area of the smaller rectangle $= 10 \times 4 = 40$

Area of the non-shaded region $= 192 - 40 = 152$

16) Choice E is correct

In the figure angle A is labeled $(3x - 2)$ and it measures 37. Thus, $3x - 2 = 37$ and $3x = 39$ or $x = 13$. That means that angle B, which is labeled $(5x)$, must measure $5 \times 13 = 65$.

Since the three angles of a triangle must add up to 180,

$37 + 65 + y - 8 = 180$, then: $y + 94 = 108 \rightarrow y = 180 - 94 = 86$

17) Choice D is correct

Let's find the mean (average), mode and median of the number of cities for each type of pollution. Number of cities for each type of pollution: $6, 3, 4, 9, 8$

$$average\ (mean) = \frac{sum\ of\ terms}{number\ of\ terms} = \frac{6+3+4+9+8}{5} = \frac{30}{5} = 6$$

The Median is the number in the middle. To find median, first list numbers in order from smallest to largest. $3, 4, 6, 8, 9$. The median of the data is 6.

Mode is the number which appears most often in a set of numbers. Therefore, there is no mode in the set of numbers. Median = Mean, then, $a = c$

18) Choice A is correct

Percent of cities in the type of pollution A: $\frac{6}{10} \times 100 = 60\%$

Percent of cities in the type of pollution C: $\frac{4}{10} \times 100 = 40\%$

Percent of cities in the type of pollution D: $\frac{9}{10} \times 100 = 90\%$

19) Choice A is correct

Let the number of cities should be added to type of pollutions B be x. Then:

$\frac{x + 3}{8} = 0.625 \rightarrow x + 3 = 8 \times 0.625 \rightarrow x + 3 = 5 \rightarrow x = 2$

20) Choice E is correct

Let x be total number of cards in the box, then number of red cards is: $x - 246$

The probability of choosing a red card is one third. Then: $probability = \frac{1}{3} = \frac{x-246}{x}$

Use cross multiplication to solve for x.

$x \times 1 = 3(x - 246) \rightarrow x = 3x - 738 \rightarrow 2x = 738 \rightarrow x = 369$

21) Choice C is correct

Subtract $\frac{1}{6b}$ and $\frac{1}{b^2}$ from both sides of the equation. Then:

$\frac{1}{6b^2} + \frac{1}{6b} = \frac{1}{b^2} \rightarrow \frac{1}{6b^2} - \frac{1}{b^2} = -\frac{1}{6b}$

Multiply both numerator and denominator of the fraction $\frac{1}{b^2}$ by 6. Then:

$\frac{1}{6b^2} - \frac{6}{6b^2} = -\frac{1}{6b}$

Simplify the first side of the equation: $-\frac{5}{6b^2} = -\frac{1}{6b}$

Use cross multiplication method: $30b = 6b^2 \rightarrow 30 = 6b \rightarrow b = 5$

22) Choice C is correct

y is the intersection of the three circles. Therefore, it must be odd (from circle A), negative (from circle B), and multiple of 5 (from circle C).

From the choices provided, only -5 is odd, negative and multiple of 5.

23) Choice D is correct

Solve for x. $-2 \le 2x - 4 < 2 \Rightarrow$ Add 4 to all sides: $-2 + 4 \le 2x - 4 + 4 < 2 + 4 \Rightarrow$

$2 \le 2x < 6$. Divide all sides by 2: $1 \le x < 3$, Choice D represent this inequality.

24) Choice B is correct

Recall that the formula for the average is: $Average = \frac{sum\ of\ data}{number\ of\ data}$

First, compute the total weight of all balls in the basket: $25\ g = \frac{total\ weight}{20\ balls}$

$total\ weight = 25\ g \times 20 \rightarrow total\ weight = 500\ g$.

Next, find the total weight of the 5 largest balls:

$40\ g = \frac{total\ weight}{5\ marbles} \rightarrow total\ weight = 40\ g \times 5 \rightarrow total\ weight = 200\ g$

The total weight of the heaviest balls is $200\ g$. Then, the total weight of the remaining 15 balls is $300\ g$: $500\ g - 200\ g = 300\ g$.

The average weight of the remaining balls: $Average = \frac{300\ g}{15\ marbles} = 20\ g$ per ball

25) Choice A is correct

In the stadium the ratio of home fans to visiting fans in a crowd is $5:7$. Therefore, total number of fans must be divisible by $12: 5 + 7 = 12$.

Let's review the choices:

A. $12{,}324 \rightarrow 12{,}324 \div 12 = 1{,}027$

B. $42{,}326 \rightarrow 42{,}326 \div 12 = 3{,}527.166$

C. $44{,}566 \rightarrow 44{,}566 \div 12 = 3{,}713.833$

D. $66{,}812 \rightarrow 66{,}812 \div 12 = 5{,}567.666$

E. $69{,}752 \rightarrow 69{,}752 \div 12 = 5{,}812.666$

Only choice A when divided by 12 results a whole number.

26) Choice A is correct

The area of the square is 595.36. Therefore, the side of the square is square root of the area: $\sqrt{595.36} = 24.4$

Four times the side of the square is the perimeter: $4 \times 24.4 = 97.6$

27) Choice D is correct

First, convert mixed numbers to fractions: $2\frac{2}{3} - 1\frac{5}{6} = 2\frac{4}{6} - 1\frac{5}{6} = \frac{16}{6} - \frac{11}{6} = \frac{5}{6}$

28) Choice E is correct

$x = \frac{1}{3}$ and $y = \frac{9}{21}$, substitute the values of x and y in the expression and simplify:

$\frac{1}{x} \div \frac{y}{3} \rightarrow \frac{1}{\frac{1}{3}} \div \frac{\frac{9}{21}}{3} \rightarrow \frac{1}{\frac{1}{3}} = 3$ and $\frac{\frac{9}{21}}{3} = \frac{9}{63} = \frac{1}{7}$. Then: $\frac{1}{\frac{1}{3}} \div \frac{\frac{9}{21}}{3} = 3 \div \frac{1}{7} = 3 \times 7 = 21$

29) Choice E is correct

Let x be the number of current stamps in the collection. Then:

$$\frac{6}{5}x - x = 100 \rightarrow \frac{1}{5}x = 100 \rightarrow x = 500$$

50% more of 500 is: $500 + 0.50 \times 500 = 500 + 250 = 750$.

30) Choice C is correct

The sum of 8 numbers is greater than 240 and less than 320. Then, the average of the 8 numbers must be greater than 30 and less than 40.

$\frac{240}{8} < x < \frac{320}{8} \rightarrow 30 < x < 40$

The only choice that is between 30 and 40 is 35.

31) Choice B is correct

The angles on a straight line add up to 180 degrees. Then: $x + 25 + y + 2x + y = 180$

Then, $3x + 2y = 180 - 25 \rightarrow 3(35) + 2y = 155 \rightarrow 2y = 155 - 105 = 50 \rightarrow y = 25$

32) Choice B is correct

If two triangles are similar, then the ratios of corresponding sides are equal.

$\frac{AC}{AE} = \frac{BC}{DE} = \frac{18}{9} = 2, \frac{AC}{AE} = 2$

This ratio can be used to find the length of AC: $AC = 2 \times AE$, $AC = 2 \times 9 \rightarrow AC = 18$

The length of AE is given as 9 and we now know the length of AC is 18, therefore:

$EC = AC - AE, EC = 18 - 9, EC = 9$

33) Choice D is correct

Let E age of Ella, we know Ella is 4 years older than Ava: $E = 4 + A \rightarrow A = S - 3$

34) Choice C is correct

Let L be the length of the rectangular and W be the width of the rectangular. Then, $L = 4W + 3$

The perimeter of the rectangle is 36 meters. Therefore: $2L + 2W = 36$, $L + W = 18$

Replace the value of L from the first equation into the second equation and solve for W: $(4W + 3) + W = 18 \rightarrow 5W + 3 = 18 \rightarrow 5W = 15 \rightarrow W = 3$

The width of the rectangle is 3 meters and its length is: $L = 4W + 3 = 4(3) + 3 = 15$

The area of the rectangle is: $Length \times Width = 3 \times 15 = 45$

35) Choice C is correct

The sum of two supplementary angles is 180 degrees. Then:

$(3x - 10) + (x + 2) = 180$. Simplify and solve for x: $(3x - 10) + (x + 2) = 180 \rightarrow$

$4x - 8 = 180 \rightarrow 4x = 180 + 8 \rightarrow 4x = 188 \rightarrow x = 47$

36) Choice E is correct

Let x be all expenses, then $\frac{22}{100}x = \$660 \rightarrow x = \frac{100 \times \$660}{22} = \$3,000$

He spent for his rent: $\frac{27}{100} \times \$3,000 = \$810$

37) Choice E is correct

To find the area of the shaded region subtract the area of the smaller circle from bigger circle.

$$S_{bigger} - S_{smaller} = \pi(r_{bigger})^2 - \pi(r_{smaller})^2 \Rightarrow$$

$$S_{bigger} - S_{smaller} = \pi(12)^2 - \pi(8)^2 \Rightarrow 144\pi - 64\pi = 80\pi \ in^2$$

38) Choice E is correct

The perimeter of the rectangle is: $2x + 2y = 30 \rightarrow x + y = 15 \rightarrow x = 15 - y$

The area of the rectangle is: $x \times y = 50 \rightarrow (15 - y)(y) = 50 \rightarrow y^2 - 15y + 50 = 0$

Solve the quadratic equation by factoring. $(y - 5)(y - 10) = 0 \rightarrow y = 5$ (Unacceptable, because y must be greater than 5) or $y = 10$

If $y = 10 \rightarrow x \times y = 50 \rightarrow x \times 10 = 50 \rightarrow x = 5$

39) Choice D is correct

First, find the measure of angle RQS. Angles RQS and PQR are supplementary and therefore their sum is 180 degrees. Then:

$$PQR + RQS = 180 \rightarrow 135 + RQS = 180 \rightarrow RQS = 45$$

The sum of all angles in a triangle is 180 degrees. Then:

$$45 + 52 + x = 180 \rightarrow 97 + x = 180 \rightarrow x = 83$$

40) Choice C is correct

x is directly proportional to the square of y. Then: $x = cy^2 \rightarrow 12 = c(2)^2 \rightarrow 12 = 4c \rightarrow$

$c = \frac{12}{4} = 3$. The relationship between x and y is: $x = 3y^2, x = 75 \rightarrow 75 = 3y^2 \rightarrow$

$y^2 = 25 \rightarrow y = 5$

41) Choice D is correct

The amount of money that Jack earns for one hour: $\frac{\$616}{44} = \$14$

A number of additional hours that he works to make enough money is: $\frac{\$826 - \$616}{1.5 \times \$14} = 10$

Number of total hours is: $44 + 10 = 54$

42) Choice E is correct

$2.5\% \ of \ 1200 = \frac{2.5}{100} \times 1200 = 30$

43) Choice D is correct

Solve for x: $x^3 + 18 = 130 \rightarrow x^3 = 112$

Let's review the choices.

A. 1 and 2 $1^3 = 1$ and $2^3 = 8$, 112 is not between these two numbers.

B. 2 and 3 $2^3 = 8$ and $3^3 = 27$, 112 is not between these two numbers.

C. 3 and 4 $3^3 = 27$ and $4^3 = 64$, 112 is not between these two numbers.

D. 4 and 5 $4^3 = 64$ and $5^3 = 125$, 112 is between these two numbers.

E. 5 and 6 $5^3 = 125$ and $6^3 = 216$, 112 is not between these two numbers.

44) Choice B is correct

15 second is one fourth of a minute. One fourth of 72 is 18. $72 \div 4 = 18$. Jack types 18 words in 15 seconds.

45) Choice E is correct

In scientific notation all numbers are written in the form of: $m \times 10^n$, where m is between 1 and 10. To find an equivalent value of 0.000,000,000,000,042,121, move the decimal point to the right so that you have a number that is between 1 and 10. Then: 4.2121. Now, determine how many places the decimal moved in step 1, then put it as the power of 10. We moved the decimal point 14 places. Then: 10^{-14} when the decimal moved to the right, the exponent is negative.

Then: $0.000,000,000,000,042,121 = 4.2121 \times 10^{-14}$

46) Choice C is correct

A. $|4 - 2| = |2| = 2$

B. $|2 - 4| = |-2| = 2$

C. $|-2 - 4| = |-6| = 6$

D. $|2 - 4| - |4 - 2| = |2| - |2| = 2 - 2 = 0$

E. $|2 - 4| + |4 - 2| = |-2| + |2| = 2 + 2 = 4$

Choice C is the largest number.

47) Choice C is correct

85% of 40 is: $0.85 \times 40 = 34$. So, the student solves 34 questions correctly.

48) Choice B is correct

Use simple interest formula:

$I = prt$ ($I = interest, p = principal, r = rate, t = time$)

Simple interest $I = 2,500 \times 0.08 \times 6 = 1,200$

She will pay $1,200 interest at the end of 6 years.

49) Choice D is correct

The two greatest integers less than -3.34 are -4 and -5. Since -5 is odd, the answer is -4.

50) Choice C is correct

Since integer x is evenly divisible by 4, substitute 4 for x in the answer choices to determine which expression is also divisible by 4: Let $x = 4$.

Choice A: $x + 1 = 4 + 1 = 5$ This is NOT divisible by 4.

Choice B: $2x + 1 = 2(4) + 1 = 9$ This is NOT divisible by 4.

Choice C: $2x + 4 = 2(4) + 4 = 12$ This is divisible by 4.

Choice D: $3x + 2 = 3(4) + 2 = 14$ This is NOT divisible by 4.

Choice E: $4x + 1 = 4(4) + 1 = 17$ This is NOT divisible by 4.

So, choice C is correct.

51) Choice E is correct

There are currently 16 balls in the bag $(5 + 8 + 3)$. Of those balls, 11 are not blue. So, the probability of choosing a ball that is not blue is $\frac{11}{16}$.

52) Choice B is correct

$ON = 4 - (-6) = 10$ units. Let $x = OM$. Then $MN = 10 - x$.

Substitute these expressions in the given equation: $x = \frac{1}{3}(10 - x)$

Solve for x: $x = \frac{10}{3} - \frac{x}{3} \rightarrow x + \frac{x}{3} = \frac{10}{3} \rightarrow \frac{4x}{3} = \frac{10}{3} \rightarrow 4x = 10 \rightarrow x = \frac{10}{4} = \frac{5}{2} = 2.5$

$x = OM$. Point O is at -6. Then, point M is at: $-6 + 2.5 = -3.5$

53) Choice D is correct

First, calculate Jack's riding time in minutes: 1 hour 20 minutes = 80 minutes

Then, convert kilometers to meters: 160 kilometers = 160,000 meters

Now simplify the ratio to find the answer: $\frac{160,000}{80} = 2,000$ meters

54) Choice E is correct

If x is the smaller consecutive integer, then $x + 1$ is the larger consecutive integer. Use their sum (-13) to find x:

$x + (x + 1) = -13 \rightarrow 2x + 1 = -13 \rightarrow 2x = -14 \rightarrow x = -7$

The two consecutive integers are -7 and -6. 2 is added to the smaller integer: $-7 + 2 = -5$, and 3 is subtracted from the larger integer: $-6 - 3 = -9$ find the product: $-5 \times (-9) = 45$

55) Choice D is correct

The relationship among all sides of special right triangle $30° - 60° - 90°$ is provided in this triangle:

In this triangle, the opposite side of $30°$ angle is half of the hypotenuse.

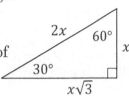 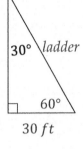

Draw the shape of this question:

The ladder is the hypotenuse. Therefore, the ladder is $60\ ft$.

HiSET Mathematics Practice Test 2 Answers

1) Choice D is correct

The capacity of a red box is 20% bigger than the capacity of a blue box and it can hold 30 books. Therefore, we want to find a number that 20% bigger than that number is 30. Let x be that number. Then: $1.20 \times x = 30$. Divide both sides of the equation by 1.2. Then: $x = \frac{30}{1.20} = 25$

2) Choice C is correct

Convert everything into an equation: $35 = (3 \times \text{shirt}) - 10$

Now, solve the equation: $45 = 3 \text{ shirt} \rightarrow \text{shirt} = \frac{45}{3} = 15$. The price of the shirt was \$15.

3) Choice E is correct

First, convert the improper fraction to a mixed number: $-\frac{32}{5} = -6\frac{2}{5}$

The two closest integers to this fraction are -7 and -6.

The integer less than $-\frac{32}{5}$ is -7.

4) Choice D is correct

Let x equal the smallest angle of the triangle. Then, the three angles are $x, 3x,$ and $5x$. The sum of the angles of a triangle is 180. Set up an equation using this to find x:

$x + 3x + 5x = 180 \rightarrow 9x = 180 \rightarrow x = 20$

Since the question asks for the measure of the largest angle, $5x = 5(20) = 100°$

5) Choice E is correct

The angle $(2x - 5)$ and 55 are supplementary angles. Therefore:

$(2x - 5) + 55 = 180 \rightarrow 2x + 50 = 180 \rightarrow 2x = 180 - 50 \rightarrow 2x = 130 \rightarrow$

$x = \frac{130}{2} \rightarrow x = 65$

6) Choice A is correct

$$average \ (mean) = \frac{sum \ of \ terms}{number \ of \ terms} \Rightarrow 85 = \frac{sum \ of \ terms}{50} \Rightarrow sum = 85 \times 50 = 4{,}250$$

The difference of 94 and 69 is 25. Therefore, 25 should be subtracted from the sum.

$4{,}250 - 25 = 4{,}225, \ mean = \frac{sum \ of \ terms}{number \ of \ terms} \Rightarrow mean = \frac{4{,}225}{50} = 84.5$

7) Choice D is correct

Solve for x. $-4 \leq 4x - 8 < 16 \Rightarrow$ Add 8 to all sides: $-4 + 8 < 4x - 8 + 8 < 16 + 8 \Rightarrow$

$4 < 4x < 24 \Rightarrow$ Divide all sides by 4: $1 \leq x < 6$. Choice D represents this inequality.

8) Choice C is correct

Based on triangle similarity theorem: $\dfrac{a}{a+b} = \dfrac{c}{3} \rightarrow c = \dfrac{3a}{a+b} = \dfrac{3\sqrt{3}}{3\sqrt{3}} = 1 \rightarrow$ Area of shaded region is: $\left(\dfrac{c+3}{2}\right)(b) = \dfrac{4}{2} \times 2\sqrt{3} = 4\sqrt{3}$

9) Choice C is correct

A linear equation is a relationship between two variables, x and y, and can be written in the form of $y = mx + b$. A non-proportional linear relationship takes on the form $y = mx + b$, where $b \neq 0$ and its graph is a line that does not cross through the origin. Only in graph C, the line does not pass through the origin.

10) Choice D is correct

Based on triangle similarity theorem, set up a proportion to solve for x:

$\dfrac{x+8}{x} = \dfrac{6}{4} \rightarrow 4(x+8) = 6x \rightarrow 4x + 32 = 6x \rightarrow 32 = 2x \rightarrow x = 16$

11) Choice B is correct

Use simple interest formula:

$I = prt \ (I = interest, p = principal, r = rate, t = time)$

$I = prt \rightarrow 600 = (3,000)(0.05)(t) \rightarrow 600 = 150t \rightarrow t = 4$

12) Choice D is correct

To solve, add the two given fractions: $2\dfrac{2}{5} + 1\dfrac{3}{4}$

The common denominator is 20: $2\dfrac{8}{20} + 1\dfrac{15}{20} = 3\dfrac{23}{20} = 4\dfrac{3}{20}$

13) Choice D is correct

Consider the case where $k = 1$

$n - k = 46 \rightarrow n - 1 = 46 \rightarrow n - 1 + 1 = 46 + 1 \rightarrow n = 47$

The list of integers from 1 to 47 contains 47 numbers.

14) Choice E is correct

The original piece of paper is $2\dfrac{3}{5}$ feet long.

The shorter piece is x feet long, and it must be less than half the length of the original piece of paper. Since half of $2\dfrac{3}{5}$ is $1\dfrac{3}{10}$ it follows that $x < 1\dfrac{3}{10}$.

15) Choice A is correct

First, find the sum of course grade of Anna, $average = \dfrac{sum\ of\ terms}{number\ of\ terms} \Rightarrow$

$80 = \frac{sum\ of\ course\ grade}{5} \rightarrow the\ sum\ of\ course\ grade = 80 \times 5 = 400$

Anna and William have the same sum of course grade, now find the Williams mean

$average = \frac{sum\ of\ course\ grade}{number\ of\ course} \Rightarrow \frac{400}{8} = 50$

16) Choice C is correct

Since both ratios have y in common, solve for x and z in terms of y in both equations.

Using $x:y = 1:3$, solve for x in terms of y. $\frac{x}{y} = \frac{1}{3} \rightarrow x = \frac{1}{3}y$

Using the ratio $y:z = 2:5$, solve for z in terms of y: $\frac{y}{z} = \frac{2}{5} \rightarrow z = \frac{5}{2}y$

The question states $x + y + z = 69$

Substitute from the two equations above and solve for y.

$\frac{1}{3}y + y + \frac{5}{2}y = 69 \rightarrow \frac{2y+6y+15y}{6} = 69 \rightarrow \frac{23}{6}y = 69 \rightarrow 23y = 414 \rightarrow y = 18$

17) Choice D is correct

Multiply each term by 3 to eliminate the fraction, and isolate x:

$-1(3) < \left(\frac{x}{3}\right)(3) < 2(3) \rightarrow -3 < x < 6$, therefore, x must be between -3 and 6. Only Choice D represents all values of x.

18) Choice D is correct

List in order the odd numbers between 5 to 30: 7,9,11,13,15,17,19,21,23,25,27, and 29. Since, the numbers are consecutive odd numbers, the mean and the median are equal. The median is the number in the middle. Since we have 12 numbers, the median is the average of numbers 6 and 7 which are 17 and 19. The mean (or the median) is: Mean $= \frac{17+19}{2} = 18$

19) Choice C is correct

Square both sides of the equation: $(\sqrt{2y})^2 = (\sqrt{5x})^2 \rightarrow 2y = 5x$

Solve for x: $x = \frac{2}{5}y$

20) Choice B is correct

The area of a trapezoid can be determined using the formula: $A = \frac{1}{2} \times (a + b) \times h$

We know: $DC = 4\ cm$, $AE = 2\ cm$, and $AD = 4\ cm \rightarrow$

$A = \frac{1}{2} \times (4\ cm + 2\ cm) \times 4\ cm = 12\ cm^2$

21) Choice B is correct

60% of students can't swim→ $100 - 60 = 40\%$ can swim.

Then: $0.40 \times 45 = 18$

22) Choice D is correct

Money received by 14 person $= \$8,400$. So, the money received by one person is:

$\frac{\$8,400}{14} = \$600$

23) Choice A is correct

There are 12 sticks in the box $(6 + 4 + 2)$. So, the probability that Emma picks a green stick is: $Probability = \frac{6}{12} = \frac{1}{2}$

24) Choice D is correct

First, calculate the area of the circle and the area of the square:

Area of the circle $= \pi r^2 = \pi(6)^2 = 36\pi = 113.04 \ cm^2$

Area of the square $= 5 \ cm \times 5 \ cm = 25 \ cm^2$

To calculate the shaded area, subtract the area of the square from the area of the circle: $113.04 \ cm^2 - 25 \ cm^2 = 88.04 \ cm^2$

25) Choice B is correct

Use the percent increase expression to find the answer:

$\frac{new \ price - original \ price}{original \ price} = \frac{5.67 - 5.40}{5.40} = 0.05 = 5\%$

26) Choice C is correct

Let x be the number of blue marbles. Write the items in the ratio as a fraction:

$\frac{x}{150} = \frac{4}{3} \to 3x = 600 \to x = 200$

27) Choice A is correct

Let x be the number: $\frac{5}{8}x = 90 \to x = 90 \times \frac{8}{5} = \frac{720}{5} = 144$

28) Choice E is correct

Set up a proportion to solve: $\frac{\frac{5}{14} \ cherry}{\frac{5}{70} \ apple} = \frac{x \ cherry}{1 \ apple} \to \frac{5}{14} \times \frac{70}{5} = x \to x = \frac{70}{14} = \frac{10}{2} \to x = 5$

29) Choice B is correct

The area of square $LMNO$ is 16 square centimeters.

So: $S^2 = 16 \to \sqrt{S^2} = \sqrt{16} \to S = 4 \ cm$

Sides LO and NO are each a radius of the circle. So, the radius of the circle is $4 \ cm$.

calculate the area of $\frac{1}{4}$ of the circle. The area of a circle is $A = \pi r^2$. So the area of the $\frac{1}{4}$ of the circle, in square centimeters, is $\frac{1}{4}A = \frac{1}{4}\pi r^2 = \frac{1}{4}\pi(4)^2 = \frac{1}{4}\pi(16) = 4\pi$. For calculating the area of shaded region, subtract area of $\frac{1}{4}$ of the circle from area of square. The area of the shaded par: $16 - 4\pi$: and $\pi = 3.14$, then, the answer is:

$16 - 4\pi = 16 - 12.56 = 3.44$

30) Choice D is correct

$2m = n + 5 \rightarrow m = \frac{n+5}{2}$. Substitute each value of n to find the values of m:

$$m = \frac{5+5}{2} = \frac{10}{2} = 5$$

$$m = \frac{3+5}{2} = \frac{8}{2} = 4$$

$$m = \frac{7+5}{2} = \frac{12}{2} = 6$$

The set of m is $\{5, 4, 6\}$

31) Choice B is correct

Plug in 25 for x in the equation.

A. $x + 10 = 40 \rightarrow 25 + 10 \neq 40$

B. $4x = 100 \rightarrow 4(25) = 100$

C. $3x = 70 \rightarrow 3(25) \neq 70$

D. $\frac{x}{2} = 12 \rightarrow \frac{25}{2} \neq 12$

E. $\frac{x}{3} = 8 \rightarrow \frac{25}{3} \neq 8$

Only choice B is correct.

32) Choice D is correct

Jack scored a mean of 80 per test. In the first 4 tests, the sum of scores is:

$80 \times 4 = 320$. Now, calculate the mean over the 5 tests: $\frac{320+90}{5} = \frac{410}{5} = 82$

33) Choice A is correct

Volume of the cube is less than $64\ m^3$. Use the formula of volume of cubes.

Volume $= (one\ side)^3 \Rightarrow 64 = (one\ side)^3$. Find the cube root of both sides.

$64 = (one\ side)^3 \rightarrow one\ side = \sqrt[3]{64} = 4\ m$

Then: $4 =$ one side. The side of the cube is less than 4. Only choice A is less than 4.

34) Choice C is correct

First draw an isosceles triangle. Remember that two legs of the triangle are equal.

Let put a for the legs. Then:

$a = 6 \Rightarrow$ Area of the triangle is $= \frac{1}{2}(6 \times 6) = \frac{36}{2} = 18 \ cm^2$

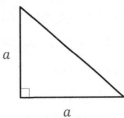

35) Choice C is correct

Solve for x: $0.00104 = \frac{104}{x}$, multiply both sides by x, $(0.00104)(x) = \frac{104}{x}(x)$.

Simplify: $0.00104x = 104$. Divide both side by 0.00104: $\frac{0.00104x}{0.00104} = \frac{104}{0.00104}$, simplify

$x = \frac{104}{0.00104} = 100,000$

36) Choice E is correct

The number of cards in the bag is 15.

$Probability = \frac{number \ of \ desired \ outcomes}{number \ of \ total \ outcomes} = \frac{1}{15}$

37) Choice D is correct

The equation of a line is in the form of $y = mx + b$, where m is the slope of the line and b is the $y - intercept$ of the line. Two points $(4, 3)$ and $(3, 2)$ are on line A. Therefore, the slope of the line A is: $m = \frac{y_2 - y_1}{x_2 - x_1} = \frac{2-3}{3-4} = \frac{-1}{-1} = 1$

The slope of line A is 1. Thus, the formula of the line A is: $y = x + b$, choose a point and plug in the values of x and y in the equation to solve for b. Let's choose point $(4, 3)$. Then:

$y = x + b \rightarrow 3 = 4 + b \rightarrow b = 3 - 4 = -1$

The equation of line A is: $y = x - 1$

Now, let's review the choices provided:

A. $(5, 7)$ $y = x - 1 \rightarrow 7 = 5 - 1 = 4$ This is not true.

B. $(3, 4)$ $y = x - 1 \rightarrow 4 = 3 - 1 = 2$ This is not true.

C. $(-1, 2)$ $y = x - 1 \rightarrow 2 = -1 - 1 = -2$ This is not true.

D. $(-1, -2)$ $y = x - 1 \rightarrow -2 = -1 - 1 = -2$ This is true.

E. $(-7, -9)$ $y = x - 1 \rightarrow -9 = -7 - 1 = -8$ This is not true.

38) Choice E is correct

$g(x) = -2$, then $f(g(x)) = f(-2) = 2(-2)^3 + 5(-2)^2 + 2(-2) = -16 + 20 - 4 = 0$

39) Choice B is correct

$(2x + 4)°$ and $96°$ are vertical angles. Vertical angles are equal in measure.

Then: $2x + 4 = 96 \rightarrow 2x = 92 \rightarrow x = 46$

40) Choice B is correct

The two-digit numbers must be even, so the only possible two-digit numbers must end in 6, since 6 is the only even digit given in the problem. Since the numbers cannot be repeated, the only possibilities for two-digit even numbers are 76 and 56. Thus, the answer is two possible two-digit numbers.

41) Choice A is correct

First convert 24 inches to feet. 12 inch = 1 feet, thus: $24 \div 12 = 2\ feet$. Then, calculate the volume, in cubic feet: $25 \times 6 \times 2 = 300\ ft^3$

42) Choice C is correct

Use properties of equations to determine the missing expression.$\frac{2y}{x} - \frac{y}{3x} = \frac{(\dots)}{3x}$

$$\frac{3}{3} \cdot \frac{2y}{x} - \frac{y}{3x} = \frac{(\dots)}{3x} \rightarrow \frac{6y}{3x} - \frac{y}{3x} = \frac{(\dots)}{3x} \rightarrow \frac{6y - y}{3x} = \frac{(\dots)}{3x} \rightarrow (\dots) = 5y$$

43) Choice D is correct

First calculate exponents value, then multiplying and subtracting:

$$200(3 + 0.01)^2 - 200 = 200(3.01)^2 - 200 = 200(9.0601) - 200 = 1{,}612.02$$

44) Choice C is correct

Since 90 boxes contain 360 kg vegetable. Therefore, 1 box contains $\frac{360\ kg}{90} = 4\ kg$ vegetable.

45) Choice C is correct

Let n represent a number in the sequence, and let x represent the number that comes just before n. $n = 4 + 2x \rightarrow 84 = 4 + 2x \rightarrow 80 = 2x \rightarrow x = 40$

46) Choice C is correct

Use PEMDAS (order of operation): $[6 \times (-24) + 8] - (-4) + [4 \times 5] \div 2 =$

$[-144 + 8] - (-4) + [20] \div 2 = [-144 + 8] + 4 + 10 = [-136] + 4 + 10 = -122$

47) Choice C is correct

First, find a common denominator for 2 and $\frac{3x}{x-5}$. It's $x - 5$. Then:

$2 + \frac{3x}{x-5} = \frac{2(x-5)}{x-5} + \frac{3x}{x-5} = \frac{2x-10+3x}{x-5} = \frac{5x-10}{x-5}$. Now, multiply the numerator and denominator of $\frac{3}{5-x}$ by -1. Then: $\frac{3\times(-1)}{(5-x)\times(-1)} = \frac{-3}{x-5}$. Rewrite the expression: $\frac{5x-10}{x-5} = \frac{-3}{x-5}$. Since the denominators of both fractions are equal, then, the numerators must be equal.

$5x - 10 = -3 \rightarrow 5x = 7 \rightarrow x = \frac{7}{5}$.

48) Choice B is correct

Perimeter of rectangle is equal to the sum of all the sides of the rectangle:

Perimeter $= 2(14) + 2(5) = 28 + 10 = 38 \, cm$

49) Choice D is correct

$3\frac{1}{4} + 2\frac{4}{16} + 1\frac{3}{8} + 5\frac{1}{2}$. Convert all the fractions to a common denominator (16):

$3\frac{4}{16} + 2\frac{4}{16} + 1\frac{6}{16} + 5\frac{8}{16} = (3 + 2 + 1 + 5) + \left(\frac{4+4+6+8}{16}\right) = 11 + 1\frac{6}{16} = 12\frac{6}{16} = 12\frac{3}{8}$

50) Choice A is correct

One gram is equal to 1,000 milligrams, or 1 milligram is equal to $\frac{1}{1,000}$ gram.

Thus, 85 milligrams $= \frac{85}{1,000} = 0.085$ gram

51) Choice E is correct

Check each choice provided:

A. 1 $\frac{4+5+8+11+12}{5} = \frac{40}{5} = 8$

B. 4 $\frac{1+5+8+11+12}{5} = \frac{37}{5} = 7.4$

C. 5 $\frac{1+4+8+11+12}{5} = \frac{36}{5} = 7.2$

D. 8 $\frac{1+4+5+11+12}{5} = \frac{33}{5} = 6.6$

E. 11 $\frac{1+4+5+8+12}{5} = \frac{30}{5} = 6$

52) Choice E is correct

Substitute 6 for m and -3 for n:

$\frac{5-9(3+n)}{3m-5(2-n)} = \frac{5-9(3+(-3))}{3(6)-5(2-(-3))} = \frac{5-9(0)}{18-5(5)} = \frac{5}{18-25} = \frac{5}{-7} = -\frac{5}{7}$

53) Choice B is correct

To answer this question, we need to divide 28 by 7: $\frac{28}{7} = 4$

54) Choice B is correct

Simple interest (y) is calculated by multiplying the initial deposit (p), by the interest rate (r), and time (t). $360 = 240 \times 0.10 \times t \rightarrow 360 = 24t \rightarrow t = \frac{360}{24} = 15$

So, it takes 15 years to get \$360 with an investment of \$240.

55) Choice C is correct

There are 60 minutes in 1 hours. Divide the number of minutes by the number of minutes in 1 hour: $\frac{1,800}{60} = 30$ hours

... So Much More Online!

Effortless Math Online HiSET Math Center offers a complete study program, including the following:

- ✓ Step-by-step instructions on how to prepare for the HiSET Math test

- ✓ Numerous HiSET Math worksheets to help you measure your math skills

- ✓ Complete list of HiSET Math formulas

- ✓ Video lessons for HiSET Math topics

- ✓ Full-length HiSET Math practice tests

- ✓ And much more...

No Registration Required.

Receive the PDF version of this book or get another FREE book!

Thank you for using our Book!

Do you LOVE this book?

Then, you can get the PDF version of this book or another book absolutely FREE!

Please email us at:

info@EffortlessMath.com

for details.

Author's Final Note

I hope you enjoyed reading this book. You've made it through the book! Great job!

First of all, thank you for purchasing this practice book. I know you could have picked any number of books to help you prepare for your HiSET Math test, but you picked this book and for that I am extremely grateful.

It took me years to write this workbook for the HiSET Math because I wanted to prepare a comprehensive HiSET Math workbook to help test takers make the most effective use of their valuable time while preparing for the test.

After teaching and tutoring math courses for over a decade, I've gathered my personal notes and lessons to develop this practice book. It is my greatest hope that the exercises in this book could help you prepare for your test successfully.

If you have any questions, please contact me at reza@effortlessmath.com and I will be glad to assist. Your feedback will help me to greatly improve the quality of my books in the future and make this book even better. Furthermore, I expect that I have made a few minor errors somewhere in this book. If you think this to be the case, please let me know so I can fix the issue as soon as possible.

If you enjoyed this book and found some benefit in reading this, I'd like to hear from you and hope that you could take a quick minute to post a review on the book's Amazon page. To leave your valuable feedback, please visit: amzn.to/349IowX

Or scan this QR code.

I personally go over every single review, to make sure my books really are reaching out and helping students and test takers. Please help me help HiSET Math test takers, by leaving a review!

I wish you all the best in your future success!

Reza Nazari

Math teacher and author

Made in United States
North Haven, CT
29 April 2022

18730815R00115